PANCAKES AND PLUM PUDDING

PANCAKES AND PLUM PUDDING

A Pathway to the Past (Looking at Customs, Cooking, Saints' Days and Superstitions)

ELIZABETH WOOD

Matador
9 Priory Business Park,
Wistow Road, Kibworth Beauchamp,
Leicestershire. LE8 0RX
Tel: 0116 279 2299
Email: books@troubador.co.uk
Web: www.troubador.co.uk/matador
Twitter: @matadorbooks

ISBN 978 1838592 875

British Library Cataloguing in Publication Data.
A catalogue record for this book is available from the British Library.

Printed and bound in the UK by TJ International, Padstow, Cornwall
Typeset in 15pt Minion Pro by Troubador Publishing Ltd, Leicester, UK

Matador is an imprint of Troubador Publishing Ltd

Acknowledgements

I would like to record my thanks to the staff of the Northamptonshire Libraries and the Northamptonshire Record Office for their help and interest.

I would also like to thank the Editor of 'Home and Country' (which has now become 'WI Life') for printing an appeal for recipes. I am especially grateful to the many members of the National Federation of Women's Institutes who wrote long and interesting letters telling me of the recipes, traditions and customs in different parts of the country. Many are traditional recipes you will be familiar with but they have not been tested.

Elizabeth Wood.

Author's Note

I began writing this book in 1979. I had always been fascinated in learning about how people cooked and lived in the days before our houses had electricity, freezers, tinned food, etc, and as a journalist, I was asked to write some articles on the subject. I had not given these a thought for nearly 40 years, but now, (as a retired priest living in a Church of England community) I have found time to explore the possibility of publishing the articles as a book.

Encouraged by my daughter Rachel I decided that it would be a pity not to pass these on to my Grandchildren, who may find them of interest when they are older.

I therefore dedicate this book to my children Charles, Rachel and Hugh.
My Grandchildren Finn, Elliot, Felicity, Yianni, Penelope, Mary and Magnus.
And my late Husband, John Comely Wood
who always encouraged me in my work.

Elizabeth Wood.

Foreword

A century or so ago it was possible to look at the food on one's plate and know more or less what the date was. Not only were a large number of foods confined to a short season, but there were so many church and other festivals, each with its own recipes, that one would often know the exact day.

This seasonal aspect has almost disappeared from our food, Canning, freezing and quick-drying have made fruit and vegetables available all the year round, and with the decline in the Church's influence the old festivals have lost their meaning.

With the exception of Christmas, which is universally celebrated, one scarcely notices the various feasts and seasons as they pass. Now that Whitsuntide is no longer a public holiday only churchgoers are aware that it occurs, and most of us find it difficult to remember to make pancakes on Shrove Tuesday or hot cross buns on Good Friday. Yet there was a time when the Book of Common Prayer was so familiar that gardeners planted their crops by it and recipes contained such instruction as 'beat for as long as it takes to recite the Magnificat'.

People measured out their lives by the Saints' Days and would choose an auspicious day for an important undertaking. This ancient custom has not been quite forgotten. Newly engaged couples often wait until Christmas to tell their friends, such news being too momentous to announce on an ordinary day.

It is interesting to look back at some of the old festive dishes and customs and consider their origins. Most of the Christian festivals coincide with much earlier religious festivals, some dating back to Pagan and Celtic times. Realising how important they were as seasons of rejoicing or remembrance, the early church wisely allowed the people to continue with their customs, but added to them a Christian meaning.

Samhain, the Celtic Festival of the Dead, became Halloe'en when in 998 Odilo, Abbot of Cluny, ordained a Mass in remembrance of the dead at this season.

The Romans held a Saturnalia from 17th to 24th December. They sang, exchanged presents and decorated their houses with evergreens. The Druids celebrated the Winter Solstice with a mistletoe-cutting ceremony and the blessing of the Yule Log. Remnants of these customs still exist in our own Christmas festivities, even if the only Yule Log we ever see is a chocolate-covered Swiss Roll.

In early February, candles were carried by the Romans in honour of the Goddess Februa, the mother of Mars. We now call this season Candlemas when we celebrate Christ's Presentation in the Temple, and Simeon's prophecy that he would become a 'light to lighten the Gentiles'.

The old Pagan festivals were not all Christianised. Beltane, or May Day, which was an important public holiday until the Reformation, was not really a church festival (although it coincides with the feast of St Philip and St James). It is still celebrated in country districts where a little girl is chosen as May Queen and decked with flowers; though the children keeping up the Celtic custom of dancing round the maypole are unaware that the original was a phallic symbol.

As communities become more urban the old customs are dying out. The sense of fear at the approach of winter, or of joy at the return of spring, cannot be fully realised in these days of electric light and central heating. It is difficult for us to imagine a time with no anaesthetics, when pain and intense cold were part of everyday life. Scientific knowledge has destroyed most of the superstitions (thought we still touch wood – forgetting that this is to placate a Pagan Tree Spirit), and with ready-made forms of entertainment the May Games and Fire Festivals are forgotten.

However we can still preserve a link with the past by making the Festive Foods that have been eaten for centuries on certain dates. In this book I have tried to give a little of the history and origins of some of these dishes, and though it cannot claim to be comprehensive I think it is representative. I have included recipes (or a modern equivalent) together with some of the customs and superstitions of earlier days, as well as the festivals of some of the best-known saints. At one time almost every aspect of daily life had its own superstitions and proverbs covering birth, death, marriage, cooking, eating, farming and so on. Having no official weather forecasters, farmers and fishermen observed the behaviour of insects and animals, the colour of the sky, or the number of berries on the hedges. Many of their conclusions have come down to us in rhyming couplets or proverbs so I have included some of these as well.

It is impossible in most cases to say how old the recipes are. Although cooking methods at court or in large castles and manors is well documented, traditional country recipes were handed down verbally from mother to daughter for centuries before finding their way into the cookery books. Poor people probably never saw many of the traditional festive dishes such as Christmas Pie or Twelfth Night Cake, but they had ways of making their usual daily meal a little more interesting for special occasions. Some spice, currants and sugar would be added to the bread dough to make the Dough Cake which appears in many regions as the festive dish; or the daily suet pudding (cooked with vegetables in a pot over the fire) would have a small piece of meat enclosed in it for the treat. It is usually impossible to give a definitive recipe. I found if I asked 10 different women how a certain dish was made I got 10 different answers, most of them beginning "well *my* mother always…"

For many women the serving up of a well cooked meal to the family and their friends around the table has an almost sacramental aspect that will never be replaced by buffet suppers or TV snacks. This feeling reaches its peak at Christmas, when families try to get together and weapons are metaphorically left at the door. The familiar traditional dishes give a feeling of continuity and security that is reassuring in the age of rapid change. It would be a pity if they were to die out.

Elizabeth Wood.

January

"If January Kalends be
summerly gay
'Twill be winterly weather till
the Kalends of May."

January is named after the Roman deity Janus, who was always depicted with two faces looking to the past and to the future. The Saxons called it 'Wolf-month' because during the coldest weather there was always a danger that starving wolves might invade their villages.

Long before the coming of Christ the dark days in the middle of winter were the occasion for feasting and a rest from work. The Romans had their Saturnalia followed at New Year by the three-day festival of Kalends. It was a time when divinations would be made to attempt to foretell the future. We still regard the new year as a time for looking back at past mistakes and forward with resolutions. In Somerset a key is slipped into the Bible. When opened, the text under the key is believed to give guidance for the coming year.

January 1st is celebrated as the Feast of the Circumcision of Our Lord as it is the eighth day after Christmas and according to St Luke, this event occurred 'when eight days were accomplished.' New Year's Day is an important day in Scotland where children go from door to door begging for oatcakes.

Ingredients

- Pin head oatmeal
- Cold water
- Pinch of salt

Method

Mix oatmeal and salt into a stiff ball with water. Roll thinly on a board sprinkled with oatmeal. Bake on both sides on a griddle or hot plate. (This rather basic recipe can be adapted by adding a little fat or dripping, or a raising agent such as baking soda.)

Parties are held on New Year's Eve and it is considered lucky if the first person to cross the threshhold after midnight is a dark-haired man. This 'first footer', who is usually carrying a piece of coal, some bread, salt and money for luck, is traditionally given Spice Cake and Atholl Brose.

Spice Cake and Atholl Brose

Spice Cake

Ingredients

- 8 oz self-raising flour
- 3 oz caster sugar
- 3 oz butter
- 1 teaspoonful mixed spice
- Milk to mix
- Pinch of salt

Method

Sift dry ingredients and rub in fat. Add sugar. Beat egg in a little milk and mix all ingredients to dropping consistency adding more milk if necessary.

Atholl Brose

Ingredients

- 2 glasses whisky
- ½ pint cream
- 1 cupful of oatmeal
- 4 tablespoonsful of runny honey

Method

Whisk cream until frothy, then add all the other ingredients mixing well.

Bake at Gas 5 (375°F) for 75 minutes.

In Coventry children would visit their godparents on New Year's Day to be blessed and given Godcakes.

Coventry Godcakes

Ingredients

- 8 oz puff pastry
- ½ oz butter
- ¼ oz sugar
- 2 oz currants
- Pinch of spice and ground nutmeg

Method

Cream fat and sugar and add currants and spices. Roll pastry thinly and cut into triangles. Place a teaspoonful of the mixture on each piece and fold over into a small triangle, brushing the edges with water. Brush with water and dust with castor sugar.

Bake at Gas 7 (450°F) for 20 minutes.

January 5th brings the end of the Christmas celebrations which, in the Middle Ages, went on for the 12 days between Christmas and the Epiphany. All decorations were taken down and there are various traditions as to their disposal. In Wales the mistletoe was given to the first cow to calve after New Year's Day. This was supposed to ensure a healthy herd. In many places the greenery was kept until Shrove Tuesday and then burned to cook the pancakes. Some people kept a sprig of holly to bring them luck in the New Year and to burn under the next year's Christmas pudding, though generally it was thought to be very unlucky to keep any decorations up after Twelfth Night.

The custom of bringing evergreens into the house is very old and hedged about with all kinds of superstitions. Mistletoe was a sacred plant figuring largely in Druid rites. It appears in the northern legend of Balder, the Sun God, and in classical mythology as the Golden Bough on the oak at the gate to the underworld. Its berries were believed to have medicinal properties, being used in epilepsy, heart disease and toothache. Because of its pagan associations it is not used in Church decoration, but hung in homes as an emblem of love.

Holly was considered to be especially lucky and was often planted outside houses to protect them from thunderstorms and witches. Ivy was also supposed to protect a house from ill-fortune, and an infusion of ivy berries was drunk as a protection from disease during the Great Plague in 1665.

The Christmas tree as a decoration was popularised in Victorian times by Prince Albert, who brought various German traditions to the British Court. In German legend, the Christmas tree was instituted by St Boniface in the 8th century.

Twelfth Night used to be the most festive day of the Christmas season. A special cake was eaten containing a bean, and whoever found it was crowned 'Bean King' for the day.

Twelfth-Night Cake

Ingredient

- 12 oz plain flour
- 6 oz butter
- 3 oz brown sugar
- 2 oz treacle
- 3 eggs
- ½ gill milk
- 12 oz mixed fruit
- 4 oz candied peel
- 1 teaspoonful bicarbonate of soda
- ½ teaspoonful each of cinnamon and spice

Method

Cream the fat and sugar and beat in the eggs. Dissolve the soda in milk and add to the mixture. Beat in the treacle. Add the fruit and spices and sift in the flour. Add a bean or charms (wrapped in greaseproof paper) and bake at Gas 3 (335°F) for 2½ hours.

The 5th January was also known as Old Christmas Eve. Errors had crept into the calendar over the years, so in 1752 11 days (September 3rd to 13th inclusive) were taken out. This was very unpopular as it meant that dates such as Christmas now fell 11 days earlier and many people refused to accept this. There were a number of manifestations which were supposed to take place on Christmas Eve and people resolved to keep watch to discover which was the 'real' Christmas. Bees were supposed to hum the Hundredth Psalm, cattle to kneel down, and the Glastonbury Thorn to blossom. On 24th December the thorn showed no blooms but hundreds turned out to watch it on the night of 5th January. It obligingly sprouted a blossom at midnight and many people were convinced that whatever Parliament said, this was the true Christmas.

The legend of the Glastonbury Thorn which links Joseph of Arimathea with Britain has its strongest hold in Cornwall, where it is believed that he was a tin-merchant. 'Joseph was a tinner' appears in their folk songs and is muttered as an incantation when engaged in a difficult piece of work.

The story is that he was Mary's uncle and visited Britain several times in search of Cornish tin and Somerset lead. Some believe that on one occasion he brought Jesus with him (during his youth of which little is known), though there are no historical facts to support this tradition. St Joseph is said to have visited Britain again soon after the crucifixion to found an abbey at Glastonbury. The thorn is believed to have sprung from his staff which he planted on Weary-all Hill, where it rooted and flowered.

An interesting custom that is still practised in parts of the West Country on Twelfth Night is 'Wassailing the Fruit trees'. The Wassail Cup (from the

Saxon 'Wass hael' – Good Health) would be passed round the company and the dregs taken out to the orchard and poured over the roots of the trees to ensure a good crop. In Herefordshire the corn seed was 'wassailed' to placate the Corn Mother, and these fertility rites date back to Celtic times.

Wassail Cup

Ingredients

- 2 bottles sherry
- 1 gill water
- 10 oz sugar
- 1 lemon
- 5 eggs
- ¾ oz root ginger
- A few cloves
- Grated nutmeg
- A blade of mace
- A few peeled and roasted apples

Method

In an enamel saucepan heat spices, sugar, zest of lemon and water. Carefully add sherry and stir. Beat the eggs well and slowly add a little liquid from the saucepan. Bring saucepan to boiling point and add egg mixture, whisking until frothy. Add the roasted apples.

January 6th (Old Christmas Day) is celebrated as the Epiphany of our Lord and is traditionally the day when the Magi, or Wise Men, appeared to Christ. We are not told in the Bible how many there were, but according to legend there were three – Melchoir, 60-year-old King of Arabia, carrying gold; Balthasar, the King of Ethiopia, aged 40 and bearing frankinsence; and the 20 year old Caspar, King of Tarsus, with a gift of myrrh.

The 6th January is also known as the Horses' Holiday as they should never work on this day.

The Saturday following Twelfth Night is known as St Distaff's Day and is the day for turning out chests and cupboards. Although traditionally it is the day for women to resume their normal duties after their Christmas holiday they had a saying

"On St Distaff's Day
Neither work nor play."

to excuse themselves if they wanted an extra day. The menfolk also had a useful mythical saint to explain absenteeism after a weekend, when they would 'keep St Monday'. (I can find no record anywhere that either St Distaff or St Monday ever existed!)

The next day is Plough Sunday, the first of the four agricultural seasons of the church's year, which is dedicated to the ploughing and sowing. The other three are Rogationtide (the season of the rising crops), Lammastide (the season of the first fruits) and Harvest (the final gathering). On Plough Sunday the farmers brought their ploughs into church to be blessed before the spring ploughing, and on the following day ploughing matches were held. These carried on the tradition of an ancient fertility rite – ploughing the earth to make her bear – and young girls would sit on or touch the plough to ensure that they would have children.

January 13th is St Hilary's Day and is traditionally the coldest day of the year. St. Hilary is remembered because his name is retained in the 'Hilary Term' for the law courts and universities. He was a 4th century bishop whose life was spent helping to formulate the official doctrine of the church.

January 17th is the feast of St Antony, the 3rd century hermit whose temptations were a popular subject for medieval paintings. Statues of St. Antony usually include a pig.

January 18th is the feast of St Prisca (or Priscilla), virgin and martyr, who is represented in art between two lions who are supposed to have refused to attack her – presumably at public games when throwing Christians to the lions was a form of entertainment.

January 20th is St Agnes Eve (her feast being the following day). St Agnes was a Roman girl who lived in the 3rd century and was martyred for preserving her virginity, so it seems strange that she is the saint invoked by maidens wishing to see their future husbands. In the 16th century, girls would say before going to bed

"Fair St Agnes play thy part
And send to me my own sweetheart.
Not in his best or worst array,
But in the clothes he wears each day.
That tomorrow I may him ken,
From among all other men."

Keats' poem 'On the Eve of St Agnes' tells of a girl who makes the ritual preparations for a glimpse of her lover. These rituals vary from place to place, but have certain things in common. One is that silence must be kept for a specified time, another that before retiring the girl should eat something very salty. In many places the girls would prepare (in silence) a Dumb Cake made from flour, salt and water in equal proportions. In some places the ritual meal included salt fish. Girls were supposed to spend the day without eating or drinking, walk backwards upstairs, eat the Dumb Cake and jump into bed without looking over their shoulder. In the North these preparations would be cancelled out by a kiss and St. Agnes Eve was an excuse for young men to try to kiss all the girls.

January 25th, St Paul's Day, is a weather divining day with the rhyme

"If St Paul's be fair and clear
It then betides a happy year."

This feast celebrates the famous conversion on the road to Damascus before St Paul began his long mission to the Gentiles.

In Scotland January 25th is celebrated as Burns' Night in honour of the poet. Burns' Night Suppers are held with traditional Scottish dishes such as Haggis, Clapshot and Herring fillets in oatmeal. Quantities of whisky are usually drunk as the Scots have a convenient superstition that it is lucky to take the last drink from a bottle.

Haggis

Ingredients

- A sheep's paunch
- 2 teacups oatmeal
- 1 teacup suet
- A sheep's heart and liver
- Onions
- A little stock
- Plenty of seasoning

Method

Clean the paunch well and leave to soal overnight in salted water. Mince meat and grate suet and onions. Season well and add oatmeal and enough stock to moisten well. Fill the paunch half full and sew it up. Boil for three hours. (This can also be made in a pudding basin.)

Clapshot

Ingredients

- Boiled potatoes
- Boiled turnips
- Dripping
- Pepper and salt

Method

Mash all the ingredients together well and serve hot. An excellent accompaniment for Haggis.

Herrings in Oatmeal

Ingredients

- 2 herrings
- 1 tablespoonful medium oatmeal
- Dripping
- Pepper and salt

Method

Scale, behead and wash the herrings and dry carefully before boning them. Mix the oatmeal with seasonings and use to coat herring fillets. Fry in dripping.

February

"All the months of the year
Curse a fair Februeer."

February was named after the Roman Goddess Februa, the mother of Mars. The Saxons called it Kale-Month because by February, kale or cabbage was probably the main item on the menu. It must have been a depressing month with the countryside in the icy grip of winter, the Yuletide celebrations behind them and spring a long way ahead. The animals, killed at Halloe'en, would probably have been eaten and potatoes had not yet arrived in Britain.

It is very difficult to find out exactly what poor people ate, apart from the basics of bread and ale. Some sources claim that few vegetables were eaten until comparatively recently, but this may be because often they were not recorded in manorial accounts, being home grown. According to early recipe books, broths contained 'potherbs' and a Royal Cookbook of 1390 gives a salad which uses 12 different herbs and vegetables. Before 1066 the

peasants had been able to supplement their meagre diet with any small animals or birds they could catch in the many forests that covered Britain. The situation was much worse after the Normans came. Laws were passed forbidding anyone to hunt or take firewood and the penalty was mutilation or death.

February 1st is St Bride's Day. There seems to be some confusion about who St Bride was and she appears to have three distinct identities. The first 'Bride' was a Celtic goddess who presided over a milking festival. St Bride of Kildare was a historical figure living from 452 to 525 A.D.

The third 'Bride' is St Bride of the Isles or the Aidwoman. In Scotland women make up a spare bed on February 1st as Bride was supposed to have done for the Virgin Mary at her confinement and they pray to her to aid them in their own confinements as she aided Mary.

In Ireland square straw crosses are hung up for luck on St Bride's Day and the previous year's crosses are broken and scattered in the fields for fertility. This custom probably dates back to the earlier Celtic Bride. Dew collected on St Bride's Day was considered to be particularly good for the complexion.

On February 1st in Ireland housewives would bake a cake (Bairin-break) and invite their friends in to share it and porridge was thrown into the sea to ensure a good catch of fish. In Scotland they ate a Bride Bannock.

Bride Bannock

Ingredients

- 8 oz oatmeal
- Pinch of baking powder
- Pinch of salt
- Tablespoon of bacon fat

Method

Put the dry ingredients into a bowl. Add melted fat and enough water to make a firm dough. Roll thinly to the size of a dinner-plate and cook on a hot griddle. Serve hot.

February 2nd is the Feast of the Purification of the Virgin Mary (known as Candlemas) when snowdrops were brought into the house to purify it. It is one of the 'weather-divining' days and there are several rhymes connected with it.

"When the wind's in the east on Candlemas Day
There it will stick till the second of May."

"If Candlemas Day be fair and bright
Winter will have another flight."

"If Candlemas Day be shower and rain
Winter is gone and will not come again."

At Candlemas, girls would chase crows. Whichever direction the crow flew led to where the girl's future husband lived.

In some towns and cities the ecclesiastical mystery plays were held at Candlemas. A field would be set aside as a 'play-field' and arranging the pageants or plays was the responsibility of the Aldermen or the Masters of the Crafts. Before the Reformation there were many such pageants to relieve the dull monotony of everyday life. The Church of Rome allotted a patron saint to each of the craft guilds and they would hold a pageant in celebration of their Saint's day.

In Scotland, the first Monday after Candlemas was known as 'Mealie Monday'. It was the day the Scottish University students took time off to tramp home and refill their sack of oatmeal. Scottish food is very basic, and reading Scottish cookery books one gains the impression that 'fancy cooking' is rather despised by a people 'reared on oatmeal and the Shorter Catechism'.

Oatmeal was their staple grain and was used to thicken soups and drinks, made into porridge (which for some reason Highlanders always ate standing up) and oatcakes, which are one of the earliest recipes known in the British Isles. Originally they were cooked on the 'greadeal' or ring of stones around the fire (the origin of girdle or griddle) and were made by simply taking a handful of oatmeal, dipping the clenched hand into water to moisten the oats, and then laying the cake on the baking stone. In the 14th century every Scottish soldier carried a bag of oatmeal and a metal plate to bake his own oatcakes. Samuel Johnson defined oats as 'a grain which in England is given to horses, but in Scotland supports the people'.

Many Scottish dishes have very little aesthetic appeal – Haggis and Singed Sheep's Head being amongst their favourites. Sauces were little used but bread sauce, which they claim to have invented, is typically both filling and economical. Soups were generally made from the broth used to cook the mutton or venison, thickened with oatmeal.

February 3rd is the day to burn a candle to St Blaise for toothache.

St Blaise is one of the 14 'Auxiliary Saints' whose assistance was requested for various ills and misfortunes. His emblems are a comb or two crossed candles.

February 5th is the Feast of St Agatha. Little is known of her but according to legend she was tortured by having her breasts cut off. Pictures show her carrying them on a dish and as they have often been mistaken for bells she was adopted as the patron saint of bell-founders.

February 12th is the Feast of the patron saint of inn-keepers and circus people, St Julian the Hospitaller.

February 14th is the Feast of St Valentine, probably the only feast-day remembered by most people in Britain. St Valentine was martyred somewhere around the year 270 A.D. under Emperor Claudius II. He was a presbyter of the church and was said to be killed for marrying young lovers after Claudius had forbidden soldiers to marry, finding that this made them reluctant to go to war. Traditionally St Valentine's Day is the mating day for birds. It is also the day when young people drew lots to see who would be their sweetheart for a year. In Leicestershire young men would leave Valentine buns on their sweethearts' doorsteps. In other places girls baked a Valentine cake.

Valentine Cake

Ingredients

- 3 oz butter
- 3 oz caster sugar
- 2 eggs
- 4 oz self-raising flour

Cream butter and sugar and beat in the eggs. Sift in the flour and put in heart-shaped tins. Bake at Gas 4 (350°F) for 45 minutes. Pipe 'heart' motifs and initials in butter cream.

St Valentine's Day was another of the many occasions on which girls would try to discover the identity of their future husband. At midnight they would run around the church saying

"I sow hempseed, hempseed I sow,
He that loves me come after me and mow."

and then wait (if they were brave enough) for their lover to appear. Nowadays sweethearts exchange sentimental cards, or humorous ones are sent anonymously as a joke.

St Valentine's Day is also the day to plant beans:

"On St Valentine's Day
Cast beans in clay."

Farmers and gardeners must have used the Prayer Book as their calendar, as the traditional dates for planting crops are all church festivals or saints' days. One almost suspects that morning service on Sundays was spent looking through the Prayer Book and planning the week's work. Illogically the practice continues right through the moveable feasts; for instance, Good Friday (which can be as early as March 20th or as late as April 23rd) is the traditional day to plant parsley.

To remind themselves that 'to sow thin is to mow thin' and therefore a false economy, the farmer would plant four beans in each hole saying

"One for the rook
One for the crow
One to rot
And one to grow."

The second half of February was when geese were expected to start laying again

"By Valentine's Day
Every good goose should lay.
By David and Chad
Both good and bad"

(referring to March 1st and 2nd – St David's Day and St Chad's Day).

Shrovetide depends on the date when Easter falls and I have placed all the events between Shrovetide and Trinity Sunday approximately. It is quite easy to work out the dates of the moveable feasts for any particular year as the Book of Common Prayer gives a table with clear details. Even the most secular diary usually gives the date for Easter Sunday and one can use this to find the other dates. Count back 40 days (not including Sundays). You will end on a Wednesday and this is Ash Wednesday. The preceding day is Shrove Tuesday. Passion Sunday and Palm Sunday are two weeks and one week before Easter. Rogation Sunday is five weeks after Easter, Ascension Day 40 days after Easter, Whitsunday seven weeks after Easter and Trinity Sunday eight weeks after Easter.

At one time priests were sent to Rome each year to find out the date of the next Easter as it was a closely guarded secret. Country people had their own (not very accurate) way of reckoning it:

> "First comes Candlemas then a new moon
> The next Tuesday after is Fastern's E'en."

(Fastern's E'en was a name for Shrove Tuesday – the eve of the Lenten fast).

In some places the day before Shrove Tuesday is called 'Collop Monday' and the favourite dish was collops or rashers of bacon fried with eggs – still one of our most popular dishes at least three hundred years later.

The tradition of making pancakes on Shrove Tuesday is still widespread. In Scotland women gathered with their distaffs and cooked pancakes together, adding a quantity of salt to the last one 'to induce love-dreams' when placed under the pillow.

At Olney in Buckinghamshire, a Pancake Race is still held each year when housewives run to the church in their aprons, tossing their pancakes. The winner receives a new pan, a Prayer Book and a kiss from the sexton.

Pancakes

INGREDIENTS

- 8 oz plain flour
- 2 eggs
- 1 pint of milk
- Pinch of Salt
- Cooking fat

Method

Put flour and salt into a basin making a well in the centre. Break eggs into it and add a little milk. Gradually beat until smooth while adding milk. When smooth, beat well and then add the rest of the milk. Heat a little fat in a frying pan until just smoking and then run a little batter to coat the bottom of the pan thinly. Cook until the pancake moves freely when you shake the pan. Toss or turn and cook the other side. Serve very hot sprinkled with lemon juice and sugar and rolled up.

Shrove Tuesday was the last day before Lent – the day to confess and be shriven. At one time it was a day for feasting and games as a last fling before the austerities of Lent. The Pancake Bell would ring at 11am to call everyone to confession and the rest of the day was a holiday. In some countries Shrovetide is still kept as a Carnival, in fact the word is derived from 'carne vale' or 'farewell to meat'.

Various reasons are given for the custom of making pancakes. It may have been to sustain the people in their long wait to be shriven but it is more likely that it was to use up the eggs and fat that were forbidden during Lent. Originally fasting was very strict and dairy products, meat and fish were forbidden. Since there can have been little fruit or vegetables by February there was not much to eat besides bread. Later the rules were relaxed until only meat was forbidden. Early recipe books show beaver as a lenten dish. Perhaps as it could swim our forefathers chose to designate it a fish so that they could eat it during Lent!

On Shrove Tuesday girls always brought out their skipping ropes and boys their tops. It has always been a mystery to me how, as children, we knew when it was time to change from playing skipping to marbles, or marbles to tops. Apart from 'conkers' (played with horse chestnuts) there seems no reason why the other games should only be played between certain dates. Although I always took a ball or hopscotch stone to school when others did, I never discovered who decreed that we should change games.

In Scotland Shrove Tuesday was the traditional day for cock-fighting. The loser generally found its way into Cock-a-Leekie Soup.

Cock-a-Leekie Soup

Ingredients

- One cock
- 2 pounds of leeks
- 4 pints of stock
- Seasoning

Method

Place fowl in a large pan with chopped leeks, stock and seasoning. Bring to boil and simmer for three hours.

At Earls Barton in Northamptonshire Leek Pie is still the traditional dish for Shrove Tuesday as it has been for many years.

Ingredients

- 8 oz flour
- 5 oz lard
- ¾ lb beef steak
- ¾ lb fresh rowey pork
- 1 lb of leeks
- Seasoning

Method

Stew the pork and beef in the oven and allow to cool before removing fat. Wash, slice and boil the leeks. Make pastry with the flour, lard and a little water. Fill a pie-dish with alternate layers of meat and leeks topping it with a layer of leeks. Pour on a little of the meat gravy and cover with pastry. Bake at Gas 7 (450°F) for 25 minutes.

In Bedfordshire large quantities of doughnuts were eaten at Shrovetide.

Bedfordshire Doughnuts

Ingredients

- 8 oz flour
- 2 oz butter
- ½ gill milk
- 1 oz caster sugar
- ½ oz yeast
- 1 egg
- Raspberry jam
- Fat for frying

Method

Rub the fat into flour. Cream the yeast with 1 teaspoonful of sugar and add warmed milk. Leave for a few minutes then add beaten eggs and pour mixture into flour and add rest of sugar. Leave to rise. Form 12 balls and leave for 10 minutes. Make a well in each and fill with jam, closing hole up again. Heat fat and cook doughnuts for eight minutes. Toss in sugar and cinnamon.

The night before Shrove Tuesday is known as Pan Shard Night in Somerset. Youths throw stones and pots at people's doors and if caught have their faces blackened.

Ash Wednesday is the day following Shrove Tuesday and marks the first day of Lent, the period set aside by the church for fasting and self-denial. It has been called Ash Wednesday since 1099 and on this day the priests mark a cross on the foreheads of the faithful with a finger dipped in ashes. Palm Crosses from the previous year are burnt and the ashes used for this purpose. Ashes have been a token of sorrow and repentance since Old Testament times. For some strange reason Ash Wednesday was once known as Cursing Day, as up to mid-day men were allowed to swear unreproved. Children who neglected to wear a sprig of ash were pinched or pushed into nettles.

In Lancashire it is known as Fritter Wednesday and they eat Ash Wednesday Fritters.

Ash Wednesday Fritters

Ingredients

- ¾ oz yeast
- ½ pint warm milk
- 1 oz lard
- 12 oz plain flour
- 3 oz currants
- 1½ oz raisins
- Pinch mixed spice
- 1 tablesoonful of sugar
- 1 chopped apple

Method

Put yeast in lukewarm milk and leave for 20 minutes. Melt lard and add to mixture. Sift in flour and add other dry ingredients. Add fruit. Fry in spoonfuls until golden brown on both sides. Serve hot sprinkled with sugar.

February has always been the month for purification. The word 'februare' means to expiate or to purify and the Feast of the Purification of the Virgin Mary takes place in February. To purify the blood at this time of the year our ancestors would eat Nettle Soup.

Nettle Soup

Ingredients

- 2 cups of young nettle tops
- ¼ cup of bacon fat
- ½ cup of oats
- 1 quart of stock

Gather nettles carefully wearing gloves and be sure to pick ones with a round hairy stem, not square-stemmed. Cut very finely. Fry oats in the fat until crisp. Add stock, nettle tops and seasoning. Bring to boil and simmer for 30 minutes. Sieve or blend, reheat and correct seasoning.

February 25th is the Feast of St Walburga. She was an 8th century nun who joined St Boniface in Germany as a missionary. Her feast is forgotten in Britain (her homeland) but her name has become associated with witchcraft in Germany where a Witches' Sabbath is held on 1st May which they call 'Walpurgis Night'.

March

"March winds and April showers
Bring forth May flowers."

March is dedicated to Mars, the god of war. At one time it was the first month of the year and this accounts for the names of the last four months – September (7th), October (8th), November (9th) and December (10th).

The Saxon name for March was 'lenctmonat' or length-month because the days were lengthening and the word 'Lent' is derived from this. Traditionally it 'comes in like a lion and goes out like a lamb.'

March 1st is dedicated to St David (or Dewi), the Patron Saint of Wales, and on this day many Welshmen wear a leek or a daffodil which is recognised as the Welsh national emblem. There seems to be some doubt as to the origin of this. Some books state that St David ordered his soldiers to wear leeks as a distinguishing mark in battle, while others advance the theory that these two green and white stemmed plants were chosen as being the colours in Henry Tudor's coat-of-arms. Although there are plenty of legends about him they are generally written off as historically worthless like most of the more colourful stories of the saints. Although I have not found a particular St David's Day dish, I am told by a member of the local Welsh Society that they always include leeks in their menu for St David's Day. As a compliment to the saint, here is a Welsh Leek and Oatmeal Soup.

Leek and Oatmeal Soup

Ingredients

- 2 lbs leeks
- 2 tablespoons oatmeal
- 2 pints stock
- 1 oz butter
- Salt and pepper

Method

Wash leeks well and chop. Fry gently in butter until soft. Add stock and seasoning and bring to boil. Add oatmeal and simmer for one hour. (This is also very good if made using 1 ½ pints of stock and adding ½ pint of milk after one hour and then re-heating. Served with croutons or diced crispy bacon it makes a filling supper dish.)

March 1st is the day to sow oats

"On St. David's Day
Put oats in the clay."

and also the day fleas are said to appear in houses as 'On St. David's Day the devil shakes a bag of fleas outside each door'.

March 11th marks the beginning of the mackerel season. There was a tradition amongst fishermen that mackerel must not be taken until Balaam's Ass speaks in church. The lesson for March 11th is the story of Balaam's Ass in Numbers 22.

Summer used to be the fishing season and ways had to be found to cope with a glut of fish so that none should be wasted. Wind drying was used first and later (possibly by accident) it was discovered that smoking not only preserved fish more efficiently but gave it a good flavour. Salting was used too but this was very expensive as salt-winning in our climate was not easy. Baked bricks were soaked in sea water and then heated until they were dry when the salt could be scraped off. Later cheaper salt could be obtained from the Continent where solar heat was used, or from salt mines.

March 12th is the Feast of St Gregory, the 6th century Pope who sent St Augustine as a missionary to England. It was said that he saw fair-haired Saxon youths being sold as slaves in the markets of Rome. On being told where they came from he made the famous comment 'Not Angles, but angels'.

March 17th is St Patrick's Day. Like St David his life story is hedged about with legends but he is believed to have died on 17th March 461 A.D. As Patron Saint of Ireland, his day is an important Irish holiday. St Patrick's emblem is the shamrock as it is said that he used this leaf with its three parts as a visual aid when expounding the doctrine of the 'three-in-one' or the Holy Trinity.

Famous St Patrick's Day recipes are Bacon and Cabbage and Irish Mist Coffee. There is a saying that 'on 17th March everyone who is not Irish wishes that he was'. Try this coffee recipe and you will see why.

Irish Mist Coffee

Method

Heat a long-stemmed glass and pour in one measure of Irish Mist Liqueur. Almost fill with hot strong black coffee then top with cream poured carefully over the back of a spoon so that it floats on the top. Don't stir it – the coffee should be drunk through the cream.

Boiled Bacon and Cabbage

Ingredients

- 2 lbs boiling bacon
- 1 cabbage

Soak bacon for 12 hours. Change the water and simmer for 1 ½ hours. Take the bacon out of the water and boil shredded cabbage in it for 15 minutes. Serve the bacon hot with the cabbage.

March 21st is the Feast of St Benedict whose Holy Rule is followed by the Benedictine monks. His emblems are a broken cup and a raven. St Benedict's Day reminded farmers that it was time their peas were sown

"If peas are not sown by Benedick
They had better stay in the rick."

Mothering Sunday or Refreshment Sunday is the Fourth Sunday in Lent.

The Gospel for the day is the miracle of the feeding of the five thousand, and the day was a slight alleviation from the austere Lenten fast. In 1216, Pope Innocent Ill said, "On this Sunday, which marks the middle of Lent, a measure of consoling relaxation is provided, so that the faithful may not break down under the severe strain of the Lenten fast, but may continue to bear the restrictions with a refreshed and easier heart".

For centuries it was the custom for boys and girls in service or apprenticed away from home to visit their Mother Church on that day. They would also visit their homes, carrying a gift of Simnel Cake for their mother and bringing her flowers gathered in the lanes and hedgerows. Although some church festivals (such as harvest festival and rushbearing are really Victorian revivals, Mothering Sunday and its customs have never died out.

> "On Mothering Sunday above all other
> Every child should dine with its mother."

Today many people try to visit their mother on this Sunday bringing her a gift or flowers.

Simnel Cake

Ingredients

- 7 oz butter
- 7 oz castor sugar
- 12 oz self-raising flour
- 16 oz mixed fruit
- 3 eggs
- Milk
- 1 pound marzipan

Method

Cream fat and sugar and add beaten eggs. Sift in flour and enough milk to make a dropping consistency. Add the fruit and mix well. Place half the mixture into a 7-inch cake tin. Cut marzipan into three pieces and using one third make a 6½ inch round and place on top of cake mix. Place the rest of the cake mixture on top and smooth carefully. Bake at Gas 4 (350°) for 30 minutes and then reduce the heat to Gas 2 (310°) for 2½ hours. Leave to cool. Cover the top of the cake with marzipan leaving enough over to make 12 small balls to place evenly round the top of the cake. Tie a piece of greaseproof paper round the cake and brush the top with beaten egg. Place in a hot oven to brown.

Simnel was originally the purest white bread. Now it is a cake and different towns use different recipes and decorations. Shrewsbury has a cake with a saffron crust, Bury's is made like a sandwich with the cake between pastry, while the one baked at Devizes is star-shaped.

Simnel cake was eaten with a spiced, mulled ale called Bragot.

Bragot

Ingredients

- 1 quart of ale
- 1 glass of brandy
- 4 cloves
- 1 tablespoon of sugar
- Grated nutmeg
- Pinch of ground ginger

Method

Put all the ingredients except the brandy into a saucepan and bring almost to boiling point. Add the brandy and serve hot.

In Lancashire, Mothering Sunday was also called Fag-Pie Sunday and they ate a pie made of dried figs.

Fag Pie

Ingredients

- 1 lb of short pastry
- ½ lb of dried figs
- ¼ lb currants
- ½ teaspoonful of spice
- 1 dessertspoonful of treacle
- Cornflour

Method

Stew the figs in a little water until tender. Thicken the liquid with cornflour and add spice, treacle and currants. Line a pie-plate with half the pastry, add the mixture and cover with the rest of the pastry. Bake at Gas 7 (425°F) for 30 minutes.

March 25th, Lady Day, celebrates the Feast of the Annunciation, when Gabriel appeared to the Virgin Mary. It was considered unlucky if this fell on a Sunday

"When Our Lord's Day falls in Our Lady's lap
England will meet with a sad mishap."

Passion Sunday, the fifth Sunday in Lent, is also known in some places as Car Sunday. In Northumbria people eat carlins (a type of lentil) and there is a legend of a ship carrying carlins arriving on Passion Sunday to relieve a famine. A Yorkshire lady sent me this recipe.

Carlins

Ingredients

- ½ pound carlins
- 1 oz of butter
- Soft brown sugar
- Water
- Rum

Method

Soak the carlins in water overnight. Drain and place in a pan of boiling water with a pinch of salt to taste. Boil until soft but not overdone. Melt butter in a frying pan and add carlins. Fry for two or three minutes. Serve with brown sugar and rum.

The tradition of eating peas on Passion Sunday was widespread in Wales where it is called Pea Sunday or Sul-y-Pys. Roasted peas or pea-soup were traditional dishes for the day.

Pea Soup

Ingredients

- 6 oz dried peas
- 1 quart of stock
- 1 onion
- 1 potato
- A bacon bone
- ¾ pint of milk
- Bouquet garni
- Salt and pepper

Method

Boil the stock and soak the peas in it overnight. Fry onion and potato (sliced finely) in a little bacon fat. Put all ingredients except milk into a large saucepan and simmer for three hours. Take out the bouquet garni and either seive the vegetables or put them into an electric blender. Stir in the milk and re-heat.

Because no meat could be eaten during Lent there are many old recipes for meatless pies and puddings for this time. I have included three. One, a Cambridgeshire Lent Pie, though meatless is hardly frugal and is not what one associates with a season of self-denial. The others are a Lent Pudding (an egg custard with breadcrumbs and currants) and a Lent Fish Pie which, like so many old recipes, is both savoury and sweet. It is often difficult looking at some of these dishes to decide which they are meant to be as meat and fish dishes often had iced sugar lids and other recipes included both pepper and sugar.

Cambridgeshire Lent Pie

Ingredients

- 1 dozen eggs
- 1 dozen apples
- 1 lb stoned raisins
- 2 lb currants
- 1 lb sugar
- Tablespoon each of cinnamon, nutmeg and mace
- ½ lb mixed peel
- Juice of three lemons
- 1 pint of brandy
- 1 pint of white wine

Method

Hard boil the eggs and chop them finely. Peel and core apples and mince or grate. Mix all the ingredients together and use to fill pies (rather like mincemeat).

Lent Pudding

Ingredients

- 4 oz breadcrumbs
- 1 dessertspoonful of sugar
- 2 egg yolks
- ½ pint milk or cream
- 2 oz currants
- Grated nutmeg

Method

Soak the breadcrumbs, sugar, and currants in the milk for 30 minutes. Add the egg yolks and pour into a buttered pie-dish. Grate nutmeg on the top and bake at Gas 3 (330°F) for one hour.

Lent Fish Pie

Ingredients

- ½ lb filleted white fish
- 1 hard-boiled egg
- 1 oz butter
- 1 oz plain flour
- ½ pint milk
- Parsley
- Lemon juice
- Pepper and salt
- A little sugar
- 8 oz flaky pastry

Method

Melt the butter and make a sauce with the flour, milk, parsley and seasoning. Add fish and chopped egg. Put into a buttered pie-dish and cover with the pastry. Bake at Gas 7 (430°F) for 30 minutes. Dredge top with sugar and return to oven for five minutes.

England was always famous for puddings. A boiled pudding made from suet and flour was served as a first course in many homes to take the edge off the appetite before the meat course. (In Yorkshire a batter pudding served the same purpose.) Children would be told 'those that eat most pudding can have most meat' in the hope that they would be so full of pudding that they would not complain at their meagre meat portion. If the housewife could afford it she would add something to the pudding to make it more interesting – scraps of beef or bacon perhaps. It was known as 'a shouter' if the pieces of meat were so far apart that they would have to shout to each other. Sometimes it was served as a sweet course with sultanas added (Spotted Dick) or with jam. Sometimes a lemon would be added to make my own particular favourite – Lemon Pond Pudding.

Lemon Pond Pudding

Ingredients

- 8 oz self-raising flour
- 4 oz chopped suet
- 2 oz sugar

Filling

- 1 lemon
- 2 oz butter
- 2 oz brown sugar

Make a suet pastry and line a small pudding basin reserving a portion for a lid. Pierce the lemon all over well and place in the middle of the basin and surround it with chopped butter mixed with brown sugar. Cover with rest of pastry and steam for two to three hours – the longer it is steamed the softer the lemon will be.

Saffron Bread was also eaten during Lent in the 15th century. Saffron was one of the most popular flavourings in the middle ages although it was very expensive, as it still is. Saffron is obtained from the stamens of a crocus-like flower and turns any dish it is included in a bright yellow. It was used mainly to colour egg custards and cakes or to 'endore' poultry. Endoring, to gild a bird and make it look attractive, is painting it with a thick sauce made of egg yolks, sugar, butter and saffron ten minutes before the end of the cooking time.

Saffron Bread

Ingredients

- 1 pound of plain flour
- ½ oz of yeast
- 2 eggs
- ½ pint of milk
- ½ cup lukewarm water
- ¼ teaspoonful saffron
- Pinch of salt

Method

Heat the milk and add saffron. Dissolve the yeast in the lukewarm water. Beat the eggs lightly. Put flour in a mixing bowl making a well in the centre and add all the other ingredients. Knead until smooth then leave in a warm place to rise. Knead again and shape into a loaf or put in a loaf tin. Leave to rise again and then bake at Gas 5 (375°F) for 30 minutes.

April

"If showers fall in April
We shall have flowers in May."

April is dedicated to Venus. The name probably derives from Aphrodite, the Greek name for Venus. The Anglo-Saxon name for April was Eostre-month, after Eostre the goddess of Spring, and her name lives on in our Easter.

April 1st is All Fool's Day. The idea of 'fooling' people on this day or sending them on ridiculous errands is found in many countries, but its origin is obscure. Sometimes it is said to derive from Christ being sent from Annas to Caiaphas and from Pilate to Herod.

April 3rd is the day when you should listen for the cuckoo and if you hear it turn the money in your pocket for luck.

Palm Sunday is the Sunday before Easter when, since the 4th century, the church has held processions carrying branches of palm in memory of Christ's entry into Jerusalem. In countries where palm was unobtainable other plants were used and in England pussy willow is often known as palm as it was used to decorate homes and carry in processions on Palm Sunday. The blessed palm crosses are kept carefully all the year hung on the wall, or in some places in the stable or barn, to bring a blessing on the cattle and the harvest.

In many Midland counties it is called Fig Sunday and at one time everyone ate figs. My local grocer tells me that 10 years ago he had many requests for figs at this time but now it has dwindled to only two or three each year. My mother used to hand the figs round after Sunday dinner, but many people made them into a pudding.

Here are two quite different Fig Sunday recipes. The first is from a Northamptonshire Cookery Book dated 1908.

Fig Pudding

Ingredients

- ½ pound of dried figs
- 2 eggs
- ¼ pound self-raising flour
- ¼ pound of butter
- ¼ pound of sugar

Method

Stew the figs for one hour until they are tender and pour into a buttered pie dish. Beat the butter and sugar to a cream and add the well beaten eggs. Add the flour and pour the mixture on top of the figs. Bake at Gas 4 (375°F) for 40 minutes.

Figgy Pudding

Ingredients

- 1 pound of dried figs shredded fine
- 6 oz of breadcrumbs
- 3 well-beaten eggs
- ½ pound of chopped suet
- Grated lemon rind
- Milk

Method

Mix all the ingredients together with sufficient milk to bind them. Put into a greased pudding basin (or a floured cloth) and boil for three hours.

At this time of the year housewives were very busy spring-cleaning as they tried to have it completed before the Easter Feast. (Spring has officially arrived when you can tread on nine daisies at once). Spring-cleaning was a major upheaval in the days before vacuum cleaners as carpets and mats had to be taken outdoors and beaten. As a child I hated it almost as much as our cat did. Superstitious people always swept the dust inwards and carried it out on a shovel as 'to sweep dust out is to sweep luck out'.

Maundy Thursday, the Thursday in Holy Week, is the day when we remember how Jesus washed his disciples' feet just before the last supper. Since about the 4th century it has been customary for bishops, kings and priests to wash the feet of those subject to them. In England the king performed this rite, washing the feet of the same number of men as he was years old, and distributing money and food. The foot-washing has been discontinued for the last two centuries but 'Maundy Money' is still presented by the reigning monarch.

In Scotland porridge was thrown into the sea on Maundy Thursday in the belief that this would encourage seaweed (a valuable manure) to come in to the land.

Good Friday is the most solemn day in the church's year and has always been kept as a day of fasting and prayer in remembrance of Christ's crucifixion.

On Good Friday many people still eat Hot Cross Buns for breakfast. It seems likely that these are another example of a pagan recipe which has been 'Christianised'. The Egyptians made cakes in honour of the Moon which were marked with a cross to represent the four quarters. The Greeks and Romans purchased similar cakes at the entrance to the temple of Diana. It is thought that hot cross buns may have arrived in England with the Romans though little cakes were already being eaten at this time in honour of the goddess Eostre.

At one time the hot cross buns were made from the same dough as the consecrated loaves used for Mass and the church distributed them as alms. There are a number of superstitions about them. One is that they never go mouldy however long you keep them. Fishermen's wives used to make a huge batch and give one to their husband to take on each voyage as a protection against shipwreck.

Hot Cross Buns

Ingredients

- 1 lb plain flour
- ½ oz yeast
- 2 eggs
- 4 oz sugar
- 2 oz margerine
- 2 oz currants
- 1 ½ gills of milk
- 1 teaspoonful of mixed spice
- Pinch or salt
- A little shortcrust pastry

Method

Warm the milk and add yeast, sugar and beaten eggs. Sift spice and salt with the flour and rub in the fat. Add the yeast mixture and mix to a dough. Leave to rise and then knead in the currants. Form into 20 round buns and prove for 15 minutes. Brush tops with beaten egg and place a thin pastry cross on each. Bake at Gas 7 (425°F) for 20 minutes.

Other traditional recipes for Good Friday are Herb Pudding, Good Friday Fish Pie and Ling Pie. I have found two recipes for Herb Pudding. The first comes from Whitby. The other is a kind of batter pudding which includes sage and onions.

Herb Pudding 1

Ingredients

- 1 pint of breadcrumbs
- 1 pint of milk
- ¼ pound of suet
- 2 eggs
- 3 teaspoonsful of chopped parsley
- Salt and pepper

Method

Whisk eggs and add to milk, salt and pepper in saucepan. Bring slowly to the boil stirring. Add the chopped suet, breadcrumbs and parsley. Pour into a greased pie-dish and bake in a moderate oven until brown.

Herb Pudding 2

Ingredients

- 2 onions
- 6 oz flour
- 1 pint of milk
- 2 eggs
- 1 teaspoonful of sage
- Pepper and salt

Method

Boil the onions, drain and chop and mix with the sage. Put the flour in a bowl and add the beaten eggs, milk, onions and sage and seasoning. Heat some dripping in a baking tin and pour in the batter. Bake in a moderate oven for about 30 minutes.

Good Friday Fish Pie (from Filey)

Ingredients

- 8 oz of cooked fish
- 4 hard-boiled eggs
- 8 oz short pastry
- Salt and pepper

Method

Slice the hard-boiled eggs and put alternate layers of eggs and fish in a greased pie-dish. Pour over it a little of the liquid from cooking the fish with seasoning added. Cover with pastry and cook at Gas 7 (450°F) for 25 minutes.

Ling Pie

Ingredients

- 8 oz of ling or woof
- 8 oz mashed potatoes
- 2 hard-boiled eggs
- Salt and pepper
- 2 oz cheese
- 1 oz flour
- 1 oz butter
- ½ pint of milk

Method

Steam the fish and mix with hard-boiled eggs, potatoes and seasoning. Pour into a greased pie dish. Make a cheese sauce with flour, butter, cheese and ½ pint of milk and pour over it. Bake for 30 minutes at Gas 4 (350°F).

Good Friday is the day to plant parsley (which as everyone knows goes back 12 times to the devil before it comes up). There is an old saying that 'When parsley thrives in the garden, the wife rules in the house'.

"A good rain on Easter Day
Gives good grass but little hay."

Easter Sunday is the most important and joyful festival in the Christian year, celebrating the Resurrection of Our Lord.

On Easter Sunday it was the tradition to wear one's newest clothes. An old proverb says

"At Easter let your cloth be new
Or else, be sure you it will rue."

In some places 'Easter Bonnet' parades are still held.

A traditional meal for Easter Sunday was Roast Lamb or Pasch Pie and Tansy Pudding.

Pasch Pie

Ingredients

- 1 pound of short pastry
- 8 oz cooked chicken
- 4 hard-boiled eggs
- ½ pint white sauce

Method

Line a shallow cake tin with two-thirds of the pastry. Arrange the hard-boiled eggs and chicken neatly and cover with the white sauce. Use the rest of the pastry for a lid and brush with beaten egg. Bake for 30 minutes at Gas 7 (425°F).

The lamb was considered sacred because Christ is referred to as 'The Lamb of God' and it was believed that the devil could change into any animal except the lamb. Probably for the same reason lamb bones were never burned.

Tansy Pudding

Ingredients

- 1 gill of breadcrumbs
- 1 oz of butter
- ½ pint of milk
- 3 eggs
- 1 dessertspoonful of sugar
- Juice of well-pounded green tansy

Method

Heat the milk and add crumbs, butter and sugar. Leave to soak for 30 minutes. Add beaten eggs and tansy juice and bake at Gas 3 (350°F) for one hour. Sift sugar on top.

Other recipes for this season are Easter biscuits and Easter Cake.

Easter Biscuits

Ingredients

- 8 oz flour
- 4 oz butter
- 4 oz castor sugar
- 1 egg
- 2 oz currants
- Pinch of cinnamon

Method

Cream butter and sugar and beat in egg. Sift in flour and cinnamon and add currants and knead into a ball. Roll out thinly and cut into rounds. Prick all over and bake at Gas 4 (350°F) for 15 minutes.

Easter Cake

Ingredients

- 8 oz flour
- 4 oz butter
- 4 oz caster sugar
- 4 oz currants
- ½ teaspoonful mixed spice
- ½ teaspoonful cinnamon
- 1 egg
- 2 tablespoonsful of brandy

Method

Rub butter into flour and add dry ingredients. Beat egg and brandy and add to mixture. Roll out half an inch thick and cut into rounds. Bake at Gas 4 (350°F) for 20 minutes.

There is an old superstition that a piece of silver taken from the church collection on Easter Sunday and made into a ring will cure fits.

Easter coincides with a pagan festival celebrating the Spring Equinox, so apart from its Christian significance this was a season of thanksgiving for the renewal of life manifested in the trees, plants and animals.

The egg, which still plays a large part in Easter celebrations all over the world, has always been a symbol of resurrection and immortality. Resurrection, because it contains the elements of a future life, and immortality because the soul is often represented in art as a bird which flies to heaven.

The egg occurs in many creation myths. The Sun God Ra was supposed to have hatched from an egg, and eggs were a pagan symbol of fertility.

In Birkenhead, Egg-rolling was held on Easter Monday. Wickets were fixed at the foot of grassy mounds and eggs were rolled down in an attempt to pass through them unbroken.

In Greece, hard-boiled eggs are the food eaten to break the lenten fast and in all Christian countries eggs are exchanged on Easter Day. It appears to be the most widely practised non-religious custom.

In England it was customary to decorate the house with baskets of coloured eggs. In Germany they are dyed green and in other countries they are decorated in different ways. In Russia printed like ikons; in Hungary with flowers. In Switzerland tiny flowers and leaves are tied to them and they are boiled. The most extravagant Easter eggs were the jewelled ones made by Fabergé and exchanged by members of the Russian royal family.

I always dye eggs for Easter by adding colouring to the water in which they are boiled. An onion skin will turn them yellow, moss green, or bought dyes such as cochineal can be used. A little vinegar in the water helps the colour to adhere better. Patterns or children's names can be drawn on them first with melted wax or crayons which will then resist the dye.

In Poland it is the custom to decorate the eggs (called pysanki) with elaborate symbols and to keep them as family heirlooms.

If it is wished to keep decorated eggs they can be blown by piercing both ends with a needle and blowing the contents out. This is not strictly necessary. If they are not blown they may smell unpleasant for a time but the odour will fade as the contents dry up.

The second Monday and Tuesday after Easter were known as Hocktide when money was collected for church and parish use. It was a short holiday with various sports and amusements until the 19th century.

April 23rd is St George's Day. St George is the patron saint of England as well as of soldiers and boy-scouts, but very little is know about him. He is usually represented as a medieval knight and dragon-killer and his flag showing a red cross on a white ground is incorporated into the Union Jack.

April 24th is the Feast of St Mark the Evangelist whose symbol is a winged lion. This is another occasion for girls to try to see their future husbands. In some places girls would wait until midnight and then pick twelve sage leaves – one at each stroke of the clock – and wait for their lover to appear. In other places they would attempt to find out how long it would be before they were married. They would go to church at midnight and at twelve o' clock would expect to see a bridal procession pass into the church. The number of bridesmaids indicated the number of months they would remain single.

If they saw a coffin it indicated that they would die an old maid.

Most of these ‘rites’ included such acts as going out at midnight or sitting in an empty church in the dark – conditions which would put most girls into such a suggestible state of mind that they might believe they had seen almost anything.

May

"A May flood,
Never did good."

It is probable that May was named after the goddess Maia, mother of Mercury. The Romans celebrated Floralia on May Day when games were held and homes and temples decorated with garlands.

In England May Day was one of the two great Celtic festivals. Samhain (at Halloe'en) was the Festival of Winter when the beasts were brought in from the fields and most of them killed for salting and smoking. Beltane, or May Day, was the Festival of Summer when the animals were turned out to pasture.

The most important of the Beltane rites was the lighting of the May Fire. This 'need-fire' was lit by two oak planks being rubbed together by 81 men (the magical number of nine times nine) working in relays. As the sun rose the victim was killed and placed on the fire and everyone walked around it in a sunwise direction. Later the cattle were driven through the embers to protect them from murrain and everyone took a brand to light their own hearthfires. The ashes were scattered in the fields to produce a good harvest and a libation of eggs and milk was poured on the ground.

Rowan was tied on the cowshed door to prevent the witches from sucking milk from the cows.

Some of these customs died out with the Druids, but others continued until the 1850s.

There are many superstitions about the month of May. It is supposed to be unlucky for weddings and in fact at one time weddings were forbidden by the church between Rogationtide and Whitsuntide. It was also supposed to be unlucky to bring May (hawthorn blossom) into the house. A superstition that happily I can refute is that May babies are sickly and cannot be reared – not true in my case!

May Day was a joyful festival when everyone went out to celebrate the coming of summer. We read of Catherine of Aragon and Pepys' wife going into the fields to gather May dew which was supposed to be beneficial for the complexion.

Until the Reformation May Day was celebrated with Maypole dancing, archery and morris dancing, and even in London a Maypole was erected in Mayfair and milkmaids tied flowers to their pails. However, in 1580 a magistrate wrote that May Games should be suppressed 'as they tend to no other end but to stir up our frail natures to wantonness'.

In Scotland they ate a special Beltane Bannock and another traditional dish for May Day was stuffed chine.

Beltane Bannocks

Use recipe for oatcakes (see January) and form into large flat cakes with nine raised square knobs on the top. The farmer would stand before the Beltane Fire and break off the shoulder saying

"I give this to the fox; spare my lambs,
and so on to the crow, the eagle, etc."

Stuffed Chine

INGREDIENTS

- Neck chine of bacon
- Spring onions
- Mixed herbs
- Seasoning
- Flour and water to make paste

Soak chine for 24 hours. Score on both sides. Cut herbs finely and fill the scorings with them. Cover with flour and water paste and bake for 20 minutes a pound and 20 minutes over. Remove the paste and serve cold.

Most old recipes for chine recommend covering it in 'strong paste' or 'huff paste' though nowadays foil would do just as well. This paste was often used during cooking to cover meat and poultry as it prevented the juices drying out. It was not part of the dish and was supposed to be discarded. Sometimes the recipes include suet in the paste and then it was probably eaten by poor families especially if the meat juices had soaked into it.

May 3rd (The Invention of the Cross) is the traditional day to plant kidney beans.

May 12th is the Feast of St Pancras, a 4th century martyr whose name lives on in the borough in London and the railway terminus.

May 12th is also known in some places as Old May Day and is another instance of people not accepting the loss of 11 days from the calendar in 1752 (see January 5th – Old Christmas Eve). On this day garlands of flowers were blessed and hung on the bows of fishing boats.

Rogationtide is the second of the church's agricultural festivals when God's blessing is asked on the crops. The Rogation Days are the Monday, Tuesday and Wednesday before Ascension Day (Holy Thursday). The church processions held at Rogationtide 'beating the bounds' were an opportunity to re-affirm the parish boundaries and in some places it was customary to 'bump' the smallest choirboys at certain landmarks in order to impress upon them just where the boundaries lay. Many villages still have a Gospel Oak where the priest stopped during the procession to read the Gospel.

Ascension Day comes 40 days after Easter and is the day when the Disciples watched Jesus ascend to Heaven. In some places the beating the bounds processions take place on Ascension Day. Traditional 'Robin Hood' plays were held as it was a holiday.

At Wicken, in Northamptonshire, a special Holy Thursday Cake has been made in the parish on Ascension Day since 1587 when a service, followed by cakes and ale, was held to mark the amalgamation of two parishes.

The service is still held annually by the Gospel Elm outside the former rectory. Instrumentalists from the local school join with the choir for 'The Old Hundredth' (All people that on earth do dwell) before the cakes and ale are handed round (with shandy for the children).

Although no-one is likely to want to make a cake of these proportions, I am including the recipe just as it appears in the Parish Records. The Rector tells me that it is 'very spicy'.

Holy Thursday Cake

METHOD

Three bushels of flour to be made into cakes with six pounds of currants. six pounds of butter, one pound of caraway seed and cloves. Sixteen cakes of the largest sort to weigh six pounds each into the oven. All the remaining to weigh four pounds and a half each into the oven. Divide two of the largest cakes into six pieces each for the farmers and their wives. One of the largest cakes into two parts, one part to Little Hill Farm, the other part to the farm next to the church, one cake to the Parsonage, one cake to the Park. Eleven of the largest cakes into eight pieces each, these pieces for the married poor men and their wives. Twelve of the least cakes into eight pieces each, these pieces for the young men and maids. The least cakes into sixteen pieces each for the children. Seven gallons of ale from the White Lion.

Rain collected on Holy Thursday is supposed to be good for sore eyes and in some places an egg laid on Ascension Day was hung from the roof of the house to keep it from harm.

In Derbyshire, wells are dressed with flower petals at Ascensiontide, some of the most famous being at Tissington and Eyam.

Whitsuntide, 10 days after Ascension Day, is a completely Christian festival. Birth, death and resurrection all played an important part in earlier religions, but there is no parallel in pagan rites with the concept of the coming of the Holy Spirit.

At one time many people wore white on Whitsunday and farmers gave away milk to any neighbours who called for it. A gooseberry pie or pudding is traditional Whitsunday fare in some places. This 18th century pudding recipe comes from Little Gaddesden, Herts.

Boiled Gooseberry

Ingredients

- 8 oz self-raising flour
- 4 oz finely chopped suet
- 8 oz gooseberries
- 4 oz sugar

Method

Butter a basin well. Mix the suet into the flour, add the sugar and the gooseberries and mix all together with water as for a plum pudding. Put into the basin, tie down with a cloth and boil for about three hours. Eat with sugar and butter.

Gooseberry Tart

Ingredients

- 1 pound of shortcrust pastry
- 2 pounds of gooseberries
- 3 tablespoons of water
- 4 oz sugar

Method

Cook the gooseberries for a short time in the water. Line a pie-plate with half the pastry and add the gooseberries and sugar. Cover with the rest of the pastry and bake at Gas 6 (400°F) for 15 minutes and then lower the heat and cook for a further 30 minutes.

Until recently many villages held a Village Tea and Sports on Whit Monday and two favourite recipes were Whitsuntide cake and White Cheesecakes. If this custom has been kept alive anywhere it has probably moved to the Spring Bank Holiday as Whit Monday is no longer a holiday, unfortunately. I wonder which will be the next church festival to be removed from the list of bank holidays.

Whitsuntide Cake (from Lincolnshire)

INGREDIENTS

- 3 oz butter
- ¾ pound of flour
- ½ oz yeast
- ¼ pint of milk

For the filling:

- ½ pound of currants
- ½ pound of brown sugar
- 1 oz of butter
- Yolk of an egg
- ½ teaspoonful of spice

METHOD

Warm ingredients under 'filling' until the currants are soft. Dissolve the yeast in lukewarm milk and rub the butter into the flour. Add yeast mixture and knead into a dough. Leave to rise for 20 minutes. Roll out the dough in four rounds. Make a sandwich of layers of pastry and filling (starting and finishing with a layer of pastry). Fasten the edges well with beaten egg white and glaze the top with beaten egg. Bake at Gas 5 (375°F) for one hour and leave in the tin until quite cold.

White Cheesecakes

Ingredients

- 1 pint of milk
- 1 teaspoonful of rennet
- Pinch of salt
- 8 eggs (use only 5 whites)
- 6 oz butter
- 6 oz castor sugar
- Ground ginger
- Grated lemon peel
- 1 oz currants
- A little cream
- 1 pound of shortcrust pastry

Method

Warm the milk to blood heat and add rennet and a pinch of salt. When it has quite set put it into a muslin bag and drain all night. Beat the eggs and sugar and add to the curds. Add the other ingredients and put into small tartlets for 25 minutes.

I had some difficulty getting the rennet for this recipe as the local chemists don't stock it any more. However I was able to buy some in a health food shop. At one time rennet was used a good deal to make junket but this seems to have become less popular – perhaps yoghurt has taken its place as a way of making milk palatable, though the two are quite different. Although junket is sweeter, the real difference is in the sensation of eating it which is difficult to describe. Junket is very shiny and slippery and just the thing to give children with sore throats as it slides down so easily. It is very easy to make and tastes good with stewed fruit or with a little nutmeg grated on top.

Years ago Whitsuntide was one of the most popular holidays. The weather was often warm and the whole parish would join in dancing, shooting and morris dancing.

A custom that seems to have quite died out is holding Church Ales. A Whitsun Ale was often held organised by the churchwardens who would buy the ingredients and make strong ale which would be set in the church. It would be sold at a Church Ale and the proceeds used for new prayer books, church repairs or the upkeep of the poor of the parish.

Although Whitsuntide was the favourite time for Church Ales it appears that any excuse could be found for holding one. There might be a Mary Ale at Candlemas, a Lamb Ale at sheep-shearing, a Soul Ale at a funeral, a 'Groaning' Ale at a birth or a Bride Ale at a wedding. Probably this last is the origin of the Bridal Feast. A forerunner of the 'bottle-party' was the often preached-against Scot-Ale when everyone had to bring some liquor.

Probably the phrase 'scot-free' derives from this and means someone who was excused from bringing his share.

Trinity Sunday is a week after Whitsunday and there is a superstition that if you work with metal instruments (including sewing needles) on that day, the house will be struck by lightning. The traditional lunch for Trinity Sunday in some places is Roast Duck and green peas.

Roast Duck in Cider Sauce

Ingredients

- 1 four-pound duck
- ½ pint cider
- ¼ pint double cream

For the stuffing

- 3 oz butter
- 4 oz white breadcrumbs
- 1 pound of cooking apples
- Salt and black pepper
- 1 dessertspoonful of sugar
- Pinch of cinnamon

Melt the butter and fry the breadcrumbs and add finely chopped apples. Cook a little longer and then add sugar, seasoning, and cinnamon. Stuff the duck and cook it for 2 hours at Gas 5 (375°F). Fifteen minutes before serving, pour away most of the fat in the tin and pour the cider over the duck. Baste occasionally. Carve the duck into four portions and put onto a serving dish and keep warm. Put the meat tin on top of a low light on top of the cooker and add the cream. Pour over the duck and serve stuffing separately.

May 19th is the Feast of St Dunstan, the 10th century bishop and founder of several abbeys. His emblem is a pair of tongs and according to a legend he shoed the devil with red-hot horseshoes. This angered him so much that he takes care to avoid them, which is why people nail them on their houses.

May 24th used to be Empire Day (though this has been replaced by Commonwealth Day – held on the second Saturday in June). Empire Day was a highlight of my childhood. We had pageants at school when children dressed as representatives of our Empire would come and pay homage to Britannia wearing a helmet and holding a trident. We waved flags, sang patriotic songs and generally congratulated ourselves on being lucky enough to be born British.

May 27th is the Feast of the Venerable Bede, the monk of Jarrow, to whom we owe much of our knowledge of the early history of the English church.

May 29th is Oak-apple Day, or as some call it Shik-shak Day, when an oak apple or oak leaf was worn in honour of King Charles II's Restoration. The oak symbol is to commemorate his hiding in the Boscoble Oak after the Battle of Worcester. Children failing to wear this token were in danger of being pushed into nettles as on Ash Wednesday. Oak Apple Day is one of the traditions which is just disappearing. I remember it well, but my own children had never heard of it until I told them about it. Perhaps in some parts of the country it is still remembered.

May 31st is the day to look out and iron summer dresses, as our grandmothers used to say.

"Ne'er cast a clout
Till May be out."

June

"Calm weather in June
Sets corn in tune."

June may have been named to honour Juno, the goddess of marriage and childbirth. The Anglo-Saxons called it Woed-monath or 'weed-month' and those with gardens will know why.

June has always been a very popular month for weddings. Weddings during Lent were frowned on by the church and for some reason the month of May was also unpopular.

"Marry in Lent, live to repent
Marry in May, repent alway."

but a June bride was considered lucky, especially if the sun shone for her wedding. Men were advised to choose a wife on Saturday rather than Sunday as smart clothes might hide her defects. An old proverb says 'Never choose linen or a woman by candlelight' for the same reason.

Perhaps June was originally chosen for weddings because of its dedication to Juno or perhaps because the weather is pleasant. Centuries ago there may have been an even more practical reason. A couple married in June would possibly have a child in the spring and a baby born with the summer ahead of it had a much better chance of survival than one born in the winter.

Both birth and marriage are the subject of numerous customs and superstitions. Wednesday was supposed to be a lucky day for weddings. As usual there is a little rhyme about it:

"Monday for wealth
Tuesday for health
Wednesday the best day of all
Thursday for crosses
Friday for losses
Saturday no luck at all."

Many old wedding customs are still practiced. Modern brides wear orange blossom (for fecundity) and are showered with confetti as their ancestors were showered with grain (also for fecundity). Perhaps if they realised its significance, fewer of them would keep up these old customs.

Most girls still try to wear

> "Something old, something new,
> Something borrowed and something blue."

and the couple drive away with shoes tied on the back of the car, symbolising that authority over the bride has passed from her father to her husband. Well-wishers present her with lucky black cat and horseshoe symbols and arriving at her new home she is carried over the threshhold as that is where evil spirits are said to lurk.

Wedding superstitions seem to have survived longer than most and even the most matter-of-fact girls take care to observe them as they are not prepared to take any risks on their most important day.

At one time the wedding cake was called Matrimony Cake and contained a ring, a coin and a button. Whoever received the ring would be married within a year, winner of the coin would become rich and the button would go to someone who would remain unmarried.

Matrimony Cake

INGREDIENTS

For the crust

- 12 oz flour
- 6 oz margarine
- 1 oz sugar
- ¾ teaspoonful baking powder
- Pinch of salt

For the filling

- 1 lb flour
- 8 oz sugar
- 2 pounds sultanas
- 2 pounds currants
- 4 oz chopped orange peel
- 8 oz chopped blanched almonds
- 2 eggs
- 2 teaspoons ginger
- 2 teaspoons cinnamon
- 2 teaspoons allspice
- Milk
- 1 teaspoon cream of tartar
- 1 teaspoon baking soda

Method

Make pastry by rubbing the fat into the flour, adding sugar and baking powder and mixing well. Add cold water and form into a stiff paste and roll out into two rounds. Line a spring form tin with half the pastry. Mix the dry ingredients for the filling, add the eggs and a little milk to mix. Add charms. Place in tin and cover with rest of pastry. Brush with egg and bake for 3 hours at Gas 4 (375°F).

In some places this was called Bride's Pie and was decorated with a hen and eggs – again as a symbol of fecundity. Another type of cake eaten at weddings at one time is called Bride's Bonn and some sources say that this is the origin of the wedding cake.

Bride's Bonn

Ingredients

- 4 oz flour
- 4 oz rice flour
- 4 oz butter
- 4 oz castor sugar
- 1 egg
- 1 teaspoonful caraway seeds

Method

Rub butter into flour and rice flour and add sugar. Bind with beaten egg and add caraway seeds. Form into a round cake (like shortbread) and bake at Gas 4 (375°F) until light brown.

On the evening before the wedding the couple would drink Het-pint, made with whisky and hot ale with sugar and beaten eggs. At the wedding and for a month afterwards they would drink Mead – a drink made from fermented honey – and this may be the origin of the word 'honeymoon'.

Ingredients

- 5 pounds of honey
- 3 gallons of water
- 2 egg whites
- Stick of cinnamon
- 5 cloves
- One piece of ginger
- Dried yeast

Beat the egg whites and put them in a pan with the water, spices and honey. Bring to boil, stirring frequently, and simmer for one hour. Cool and strain and add yeast mixed to a paste and spread on toast. When fermentation stops seal it and leave for nine months before bottling.

Birth is also a subject for many superstitions. Pregnancy and childbirth were dangerous times years ago, and after a fatality external sources were sought to explain it. In many countries pregnant women are still kept in purdah – because people believe that evil spirits are active round her.

In England girls expecting a baby were warned not to step over a grave or to spin, as both could mean the child's early death.

They were careful to avoid seeing a hare as this might deform the child, as the hare was believed to be one of the disguises used by witches.

During the confinement all doors were opened and knots untied to ease delivery and a knife was placed under the bed to cut the pain. If a pigeon-feather bed was available the mother would be placed on it as it was believed that no-one could die while using one.

When the child was born it was carried to the highest point in the house so that it would rise in life. His right hand was left unwashed so that he would become rich and the nails on his hands were bitten (not cut) so that he would not grow up to be a thief. (As I remember as a child seeing my own mother bite the baby's nails, I asked her why she did it. She said that she preferred not to use pointed scissors near a wriggling baby, and had never heard of the superstition!)

The baby's name was kept a secret until after its Baptism as knowledge of the name was supposed to put it in the power of witches. In the North babies are still sometimes given 'handsel' containing the symbolic elements of salt, money, etc.

In Oxfordshire visitors to the newcomer were given Pepper Cake, which was cut by the doctor. The cake was cut in rings from the middle and at the Baptism the baby was passed through the last ring for luck.

Pepper Cake

Ingredients

- 1½ pounds of flour
- ½ pound dark brown sugar
- 1½ pounds of treacle
- ½ pound of butter
- 5 eggs
- 1 oz powdered cloves
- 1 teaspoonful pearl ash melted in milk

Method

Mix all the ingredients together well and bake in a cake tin for two hours at Gas 4 (375°F). (I have never come across 'pearl ash' mentioned in a recipe before, but according to the dictionary it is another name for potassium carbonate.)

Sometimes the visitors were given the aptly named 'Groaning Cake' and a drink called Caudle.

Caudle

Ingredients

- 1 pint of milk
- ½ pint of water
- 1 gill of sherry
- 1 oz oatmeal
- 1 oz castor sugar
- Grated nutmeg
- Lemon rind

Method

Put the water and milk into a saucepan and add the oatmeal and lemon rind and sugar. Simmer gently for 20 minutes then add the nutmeg and sherry. Serve hot.

One of the oddest customs I have come across is the one Welsh midwives are said to use for coaxing a lazy baby into the world – in fact I have serious doubts about its authenticity! They quietly cook some Welsh Rarebit and place it on the bed, as no Welshman can resist the smell of it. Here is the recipe for those in similar difficulties!

Welsh Rarebit

Ingredients

- 4 oz grated cheese
- 1 oz butter
- 1 tablespoonful plain flour
- 5 tablespoonsful of milk
- Salt and pepper
- A little mixed mustard
- Rounds of toast

Melt butter and stir in the flour and add milk to make a thick sauce. Add the other ingredients, heat gently and spread on buttered toast. Grill until golden brown.

It was a matter of some importance that the child should be born on an auspicious day of the week, and many mothers must have been cheered when the baby put in an appearance on a Sunday, or disappointed when it arrived on a Wednesday.

"Monday's child is fair of face
Tuesday's child is full of grace,
Wednesday's child is full of woe,
Thursday's child has far to go,
Friday's child is loving and giving,
Saturday's child works hard for its living,
But the child that is born on the Sabbath day
Is blithe and bonny and good and gay."

It was also believed that a baby born on Sunday could never be harmed by witches.

June 9th is the Feast of St Columba who founded a monastery on the island of Iona in the 6th century. In Scotland there is a special St Columba's Day Cake which is a variation of an oatcake (see January). A silver coin would be hidden in the cake and in some places the child who found the coin would be given some of the season's lambs.

In early June people in Yorkshire ate Dock Pudding which was believed to have medicinal properties. Many herb puddings were popular, probably because the herbs could be gathered free. Some, such as Tansy Pudding, were sweet, while others were made from nettles, sorrel, dock or dandelions and eaten as the main course. Nowadays herb puddings are served fried as an accompaniment to bacon.

Dock Pudding

Ingredients

- 1 quart of young dock leaves and nettles
- 2 chopped onions
- 1 handful of oatmeal
- Butter
- Seasoning

Clean the docks and nettles well and chop them finely. Put into a saucepan of water with onions and boil until tender. Add seasoning and sprinkle in oatmeal and boil for 10 minutes, stirring all the time. Stir in butter and leave overnight. Take spoonsful and fry in hot bacon fat. Serve with bacon. (Nettles and dock can usually be found growing close together. As children, if we were stung by a nettle we would look round for a dock leaf to bind on to the stung place as it was supposed to make it feel better).

June 11th is St Barnabas' Day when in some places children sing to ladybirds

"Barnaby bright, Barnaby bright
The longest day and the shortest night."

though the shortest day is actually later in the month.

June 15th is St Vitus' Day and another weather-divining day

"If St Vitus' Day be rainy weather
It will rain for 30 days together."

St Vitus, whose emblem is a cock or a dog, is invoked against epilepsy and chorea (or St Vitus' Dance).

June 24th is Midsummer Day. Midsummer was the Celtic Festival of the Summer Solstice when special fires were lit, to bless the crops. The Celts obviously loved bonfires and they play an important part in the religious rites of their four main festivals at Halloe'en, Yule, Beltane and Midsummer.

The Midsummer ritual included tying a red thread on the cows' tails as a charm against the fairies; climbing a hill and making a pile of stones on top of it; dancing round the fires, and at one time, a sacrifice. As late as the 1880's a calf was burned alive in Northamptonshire to stop murrain in the cattle.

Midsummer was yet another opportunity to see one's future husband – an exercise which obviously occupied girls' minds a good deal. Blossom had to be gathered from an oak tree on Midsummer Eve (at dead of night, of course) and laid on a cloth. Later it was placed under the pillow to induce dreams.

When in the 5th century June 24th began to be celebrated as the Nativity of St John the Baptist, the fires were still lit in his honour. It is difficult sometimes to discover whether certain rites were being celebrated with a Pagan or a Christian meaning. Perhaps the people who lit the fires were not sure either and were as little concerned with the origins as children are on Guy Fawkes night nowadays.

Paganism was not completely driven out when England became a Christian country. If the official religion was said to be Christianity people probably paid lip-service to it but continued to tie rowan on the cowsheds and wassail their apple trees to be on the safe side. If plague, murrain or drought came they would assume that the old gods were angry, and for many centuries people were either confused or chose to worship both. This is obvious from an incantation for hammering a horseshoe to a beam. Starting

> "Father, Son and Holy Ghost
> Nail the devil to this post,

it ends with

> "One for God
> and one for Wod"

invoking both Woden and the Christian God.

After St John's Nativity the days shorten and after Christ's Nativity they lengthen. In 430 A.D. St Augustine pointed out that St John said, "He must increase and I must decrease" and this may be the reason that this date was chosen to celebrate St John's birth.

According to the Northamptonshire poet John Clare

> "It is a very old custom among villages in summertime
> to stick a piece of greensward full of field flowers
> and place it as an ornament in their cottage,
> which ornaments are called Midsummer Cushions."

Wild flowers generally fade quickly if brought in doors, but if a piece of moss is used and the whole root inserted in it, it will last longer. It sounds rather a good idea for children to do to brighten up their classrooms but unfortunately children nowadays have to be discouraged from picking and pressing wild flowers as we did. However daisies and buttercups could surely be used as they are still plentiful.

June 29th is the Feast of St Peter, the Patron Saint of Fishermen and perhaps the most popular of Christ's disciples because of his human failings. In some places fishermen perform certain rites on this day and have a festive meal.

Fishermen are amongst the most superstitious people in the world. Until this century fishing was a precarious occupation, very dependent on the weather (as it still is to some extent). After a bad catch, external sources were blamed and over the years a great many taboos were set up. A fisherman who met a priest or a woman on his way to the boat would not set sail at all. If he met someone red-haired or cross-eyed he would also turn back, and if anyone on board mentioned a pig he expected dire misfortune. The sea itself was a source of terror and figureheads were carved on ships to guide them. Blood was cast on them to give them life and this may be the origin of our present ship-launching ceremony when a bottle of wine is broken on the ship's bows.

Fishermen believed that all fish should be eaten beginning at the tail as this would bring fish to shore. To start at the head would turn the heads of fish away from the coast.

Haddock is said to be the fish which furnished St Peter with the tribute money. The two black marks behind its head are supposed to be the marks his finger and thumb made when he picked it up. The bones beneath these marks were often carried in the pocket to prevent rheumatism.

July

"If the First of July be rainy weather
It will rain for four weeks altogether."

July was named after Julius Caesar whose birthday fell on the 14th. The Anglo-Saxons called it 'Hey-monath' as during this month the hay was harvested. Nodden Cakes and Harvest Drink were taken to the fields during the hay harvest.

Nodden Cakes

Ingredients

- 1 pound of flour
- 8 oz of butter
- Pinch of salt
- Water to mix

Method

Rub the fat into the flour and salt and add water. Roll very thin and cut into rounds. Bake at Gas 7 (450°F) until golden. Eat buttered.

Harvest Drink

Ingredients

- 6 oz oatmeal
- 8 oz castor sugar
- Lemon juice
- Ground ginger
- Water

Method

Put oatmeal, sugar, lemon juice and ginger in a saucepan with a little warm water and mix thoroughly. Pour over it one gallon of boiling water (stirring all the time) and boil for three minutes, still stirring. Strain and bottle

July 2nd is the Feast of the Visitation of the Virgin Mary and commemorates Mary's visit to her cousin Elizabeth.

"If it rain on St Mary's Day
It will rain for a month."

July 3rd is known as Old Midsummer Day. This was another date which was upset by the changing of the calendar in 1752 and many diehards chose to celebrate it on the original day. Girls would dance bare-foot round a white-thorn tree before sunrise to charm their lover into marrying them that year.

The first week in July is sheep-shearing time in many counties so I have included a Clipping-time Pudding.

Clipping-time Pudding

Ingredients

- 8 oz rice
- 4 oz currants
- 4 oz raisins
- 1 pint milk
- 3 oz sugar
- 1 egg

Method

Soak rice and salt in boiling water. Strain and bake in the milk and sugar until it is tender. Add currants and raisins and well-beaten egg. Bake for 25 minutes at Gas 4 (375°F).

July 14th is the last day to pick walnuts for pickling as they have to be used before the shells begin to form. The shell can first be felt at the opposite end from the stalk.

Pickled Walnuts

Ingredients

- Green walnuts
- Brine (4 pints water and 1 lb salt)
- Spiced vinegar (1 pint vinegar and 1 tablespoon pickling spices)

Method

Prick the walnuts well with a silver fork discarding any where the shells are forming. Soak them in brine for seven days, drain and replace with new brine for a further seven days. Drain again and place on trays in the sun until they are quite black, turning when necessary (usually two or three days). Pack in jars with spiced vinegar and keep for five to six weeks before using.

In the days before manufactured jams, pickles and relishes, women did far more of this kind of cooking as a way of introducing interesting flavours into what was probably rather a dull diet.

Many of the ingredients could be obtained free. The plants that are vanishing from verges and hedgerows were treasured up until this century. Children used to be sent out to glean corn, pick blackberries or gather nuts or mushrooms to supplement the daily fare. Nowadays we have efficient harvesting methods, fewer hedgerows and so many weedkillers that it is hardly worth the trouble. I remember that, as a child, a picnic generally included gleaning corn to feed our chickens or looking for blackberries for jams and pies and during the Second World War we all took baskets of hips to school to be collected for making Rose Hip Syrup for babies.

Cowslips and dandelions, elderflower and violets, nettles and rosehips, all found their way into wines, conserves and tisanes. Some of the recipes using flowers are worth trying. Marigold petals can be added to a salad, mixed with curdled milk to make cream cheese, or made into a tart. In Wales, they use whole marigold flowers to float on their favourite soup, 'Cawl'. Violets can be crystalised and rose petals made into jam. Marrow flowers can be stuffed with mince and tied at the top to be cooked in stock. Mrs Gaskell mentions violet cakes being eaten in Passion Week but I have not been able to find the recipe. However here are a few recipes using flowers.

Marigold Junket

Ingredients

- ½ cup of marigold petals
- 1 pint of milk
- 1 tablespoon brown sugar
- Rennet

Method

Pound the marigold petals to extract the juice (or use a blender). Heat the milk to blood heat with the sugar and add one teaspoonful of rennet and marigold juice. Float a few petals on the top.

Elderflower and Gooseberry Cream

Ingredients

- 1 pound of gooseberries
- 1 elderflower head
- ½ pint of cream
- 3 oz sugar
- 2 oz butter
- 2 egg yolks

Method

Boil the gooseberries in water to which you have added the elderflower and strain the fruit. Sieve and add sugar. Beat in the egg yolks, cream and melted butter and bake in an ovenproof dish for 20 minutes at Gas 4 (375°F).

Apple Blossom Fritters

Ingredients

- ¼ lbs apple-blossoms
- 2 eggs
- 2 oz flour
- 1 pint milk
- Cinnamon
- Fat for frying

Method

Make a batter with the egg yolks, flour, cinnamon and milk. Chill for one hour then fold in stiffly beaten egg whites. Dip the blossoms in the batter and deep fry.

Tansy

Method

Make an omelette and add to it any finely-chopped edible flowers and leaves that are available. Sprinkle with sugar.

(Hawthorn buds which are just about to open can be added to this dish. Although we frequently ate these, calling them 'bread and cheese' on our way to school, I have only just discovered that they are officially edible.)

Candied Rose-petals

Ingredients

- ½ pound of sugar
- ½ pint of rosewater
- ¼ pound of rose-petals

Method

Melt the sugar in the rosewater and bring to the boil. Add some rose-petals and cook gently for a few minutes. Take them out (straining the liquid back into the saucepan) and add a few more petals. When they are all cooked boil the syrup to 'softball' and dip the petals in to coat them. Dry on waxed paper and use to decorate cakes and trifles. To make them harder, dip several times.

Elderflower Champagne (a delicious summer drink)

Ingredients

- 3 heads of elderflower
- 2 pounds of sugar
- 3 lemons
- 2 tablespoons of vinegar
- 1 gallon of cold water

Method

Put all the ingredients together except the lemons. Extract the juice from the lemons and add the juice and peel to the mixture. Cover and leave for 24 hours, then strain and bottle. It is ready to drink in two weeks. (This drink will not keep very long and should be drunk within a few weeks.)

Many plants were used to make tisanes in the days before patent remedies for minor ailments. Tisanes are infusions made like tea and allowed to steep for half an hour before drinking. I have tried some of them with dried ingredients and they taste rather like hay. Here are some of the most popular:

Cowslip tea for sleeplessness
Nettle tea as a tonic
Mint tea as an aid to digestion
Primrose tea for rheumatism
Watercress tea for iron and vitamins
Raspberry-leaf tea for easy childbirth
(if drunk regularly throughout pregnancy).

Roseleaves and petals were well-dried and mixed with herbs and cloves to make a fragrant pillow and lavendar and spices mixed to make scented bags for the linen cupboard.

The revival in home wine-making has convinced many people of the worth of some of these simple ingredients. Hips and haws, sloes, elderflowers and all kind of berries, cowslips and rhubarb are turned into wine these days. What was once an everyday task for the housewife has now become a hobby for men.

Dandelion Wine

Ingredients

- 1 gallon dandelion flowers
- 1 gallon of boiling water
- 3 pounds of sugar
- 1 lemon
- Piece of root ginger
- ¼ oz of dried yeast
- A piece of toast

Method

Pull the petals off the flowers and cover them with boiling water. Leave for three days stirring occasionally. Strain liquid into a large pan and add zest of lemon, sugar and ginger. Mix yeast to a paste and spread on toast and float it on the top. Leave for two days, then cask. Bottle after nine weeks.

Coltsfoot Wine

Ingredients

- ½ gallon coltsfoot flowers
- ½ gallon of water
- 2 lemons
- 2 pounds of sugar
- ½ oz of yeast
- Piece of toast

Method

Melt the sugar in boiling water and pour over the flower heads. Add the juice and rind of lemons and when quite cool add the yeast spread on toast. Leave for six days and strain carefully into a clean container. Bottle in 10 to 12 days.

I came across this old recipe for Potato Brandy. It is cheap to make and although it is called brandy, I am told that making it is within the law. I have not tried it yet and will not answer for its effects!

Potato Brandy

METHOD

Pour boiling water over chopped potatoes. Add raisins, demerara sugar and pearl barley. Float on it a piece of toast spread with yeast. Leave for a month and then bottle.

Most early recipe books also contain medical advice and we are not the first generation to believe that 'you are what you eat'. Our great-great-grandmothers believed that 'kitchen physic is the best'.

One of the best-known proverbs regarding health is

"An apple a day keeps the doctor away."

sometimes expressed

"Eat an apple going to bed
Make the doctor beg his bread."

The doctor is now a trusted figure but at one time he was often more feared than the disease. At the time when the doctor usually bled or stuck leeches on a patient it is not surprising that home remedies were often tried first. Housewives grew a much wider range of herbs than we use nowadays (herbs with evocative names – woodruff, camomile, agrimony) and though some were for use in cooking, even more were for medicinal purposes. Pigs lard was melted and mixed with broom and gorse flowers to make a yellow ointment to heal cuts and sores, goose-grease was liberally applied to the chests of patients with coughs, or home-made poultices made with mustard were used.

There appear to be two distinct types of cure. The ones based on herbs (tisanes, ointments, etc.) which may well have done some good, and others savouring of witchcraft and using such revolting ingredients as earthworms, lice, mice and cockroaches. They were not only used by witches (who perhaps took a malicious pleasure in recommending them to the gullible) but were carefully written down for future generations.

I wonder whether some of them were especially efficacious as cures for children trying to dodge school? I think my own children would prefer going to school if the alternative was earthworm tea or fried mice.

Here are a few of the 'cures'. Many of them are for toothache which must have been the source of a good deal of misery years ago.

Snails boiled in barley water for children's coughs
Earth-worm tea for consumption
Cockroach tea for kidney disease
Poultice of mashed turnips for chilblains
Fried mice for whooping cough
Onion juice on bald spots
Snakeskin round the head for headaches
Nine lice on bread and butter for jaundice
Spiders rolled into a pill for ague
Cobwebs to stop bleeding
Corpse's tooth in pocket for toothache
Splinter from gibbet in pocket for toothache
Drink from human skull for toothache
Spit into frog's mouth for toothache

July 15th is St Swithin's Day and the best-known weather divining day:

"St. Swithin's Day, if thou be fair
For forty days 'twill rain no more.
St Swithin's Day, if thou bring rain
For forty days it will remain."

St Swithin was the Bishop of Winchster who died in A.D. 862. He asked to be buried in the churchyard "that the sweet rain of heaven might fall on my grave". This was done, but when he was canonised some years later the monks felt he should have a grand tomb inside the church. However, every time the transfer was attempted it was frustrated by heavy rain, which only stopped when the idea was finally abandoned.

July 25th is dedicated to two saints – St James the Greater and St Christopher. St James and his brother St John were apostles and fishermen. In paintings St James is often depicted as a pilgrim with a cockleshell.

St Christopher is one of the best known saints and the legend of him carrying the Christ-child across a river has led to his being adopted as the patron saint of travellers.

On the last Sunday in July a Rush-bearing Festival is held at Ambleside in the Lake District. This is a survival from the days when it was necessary to spread rushes on the floors of churches and houses to keep people's feet warm and dry. The gathering of the new rushes and the discarding of the old became a subject for some ceremonial. Nowadays children bring the fresh rushes to the church and are given Gingerbread. This must have been a very popular sweetmeat – one of my cookery books gives twelve different recipes for it. I have included two, the first from Northumberland.

Gingerbread

Ingredients

- ½ pound of flour
- 2 oz sugar
- 2 oz butter
- 1 tablespoonful treacle
- 1 tablespoonful syrup
- 1 egg
- ½ teaspoonful bicarbonate of soda
- ½ teaspoonful cinnamon
- ½ teaspoonful ginger
- 2 tablespoons hot water

Method

Rub the butter into the flour and add all dry ingredients. Beat up egg and mix with heated treacle syrup. Add hot water. Pour into a flat greased tin and bake for 20 minutes at a low heat.

Rich Gingerbread

Ingredients

- 8 oz flour
- 2 level teaspoonfuls cinnamon
- 2 level teaspoonfuls mixed spice
- 2 level teaspoonfuls ground ginger
- 2 oz raisins
- 2 oz crystallized ginger
- 2 oz ground almonds
- 4 oz butter
- 4 oz sugar
- 4 oz black treacle
- 1 level teaspoonful bicarbonate of soda
- A little milk

Method

Mix all dry ingredients and fruit. Melt butter, sugar and treacle and add beaten eggs. Add to mixture with a little warm milk if necessary. Pour into flat tin and bake at Gas 2 (310°F) for two hours.

August

"Dry August and warm
Doth harvest no harm."

August was named after Caesar Augustus, Emperor of Rome at the time of Christ. The Anglo-Saxons called it Am-monath or Harvest Month.

August 1st (or the nearest Sunday) was Lammastide or Loaf Mass – the blessing of the first fruits. In some places the young men had games and races. Yellowman Toffee was sold at Lammas Fairs and in Scotland they ate a special Lammas Bannock which was a large oat-cake (see January).

Yellowman Toffee

Ingredients

- 1 pound of golden syrup
- ½ pound of soft brown sugar
- 1 oz butter
- 2 tablespoonfuls vinegar
- 1 teaspoonful bicarbonate of soda

Method

Melt the butter. Add all the ingredients except bicarbonate and stir until sugar has melted. Boil to 'hard-ball' then add bicarbonate. Beat well and pour into a greased tin. Cut into squares.

A fine August was prayed for because bringing in the harvest was the most important task in the agricultural cycle. Although the farm labourers received little of the profit made from a good harvest they derived a great deal of satisfaction from seeing their year's toil brought to a successful conclusion. After the last load was brought in the farmer would salve his conscience for paying low wages throughout the year by providing a gargantuan 'Harvest Home' supper for the men and their families. It was sometimes presided over by a Corn Dolly. As she represented Ceres, the Earth Mother, corn dollies are usually barred from the harvest festival decorations in churches.

The Harvest Home Supper, which was spread in the barn or orchard, was usually the only time the labourers ever tasted the 'Roast Beef of Olde England'. Usually any meat they came by was from the pig kept in a lean-to sty behind the cottage.

Favourite recipes at this time were Harvest Broth, Cream Crowdie and Harvest Cake washed down with Ginger Beer or Sugar Beer.

Harvest Broth

Ingredients

- One marrow bone
- As many different fresh vegetables as are available
- Bouquet garni
- Seasoning

Method

Boil the marrow bone in a large saucepan and skim carefully. Add the vegetables and cook slowly for four hours until thick. (If potatoes are used in this soup it is very thick and filling.)

Cream Crowdie

Ingredients

- Oatmeal
- Single cream
- Sugar

Method

Toast the oatmeal and beat into single cream. Sweeten to taste. (Can be eaten with fresh or stewed fruit.)

Harvest Cake

Ingredients

- 8 oz self-raising flour
- 4 oz butter
- 1 teaspoonful sugar
- Pinch of cinnamon
- 1 lb stewed fruit

Method

Make pastry with the flour, butter, sugar, cinnamon and a little water. Roll into two rounds and make a plate-tart using the stewed fruit as a filling. Brush with white of egg and sprinkle with sugar.

Ginger Beer

Ingredients

- 4 quarts of water
- 1 lb of sugar
- 2 lemons
- 1 oz whole ginger
- ¼ oz cream of tartar
- 1 tablespoonful of yeast

Method

Peel the lemons carefully and add to the sugar, ginger and cream of tartar in an earthenware bowl with the boiling water. Leave until it cools to blood-heat and then stir in the yeast. Leave for 24 hours, skim off the yeast, strain and bottle. It can be drunk after two days.

Sugar Beer – a Suffolk recipe

Ingredients

- ½ pint of hops
- 1 gallon water
- Honey or sugar to sweeten
- ½ oz yeast
- Piece of toast

Method

Boil the hops for two hours, then strain. Add sweetening to the liquid and float the toast on it spread with yeast. Leave 24 hours. Remove toast and strain. It can be drunk straight away and should not be kept for more than four days.

Girls used to keep a Prayer Book under their pillow during the Harvest Moon to dream of their future husband. The moon, which gradually waxed and waned, was naturally an object of mystery and there are many superstitions about it. It was considered to be unlucky to see the new moon through glass and hair was cut during the waxing of the moon to make it grow thicker. At the new-moon people turned over the money in their pocket for luck, and seed planting and the slaughter of livestock always had to take place at the correct phase of the moon.

The stars were also considered lucky and children would watch for the first star to appear at dusk and recite

"Star light, star bright,
First star I see tonight.
I wish I may, I wish I might
Have the wish I wish tonight."

August was a favourite month for Agape or Love Feasts when members of religious sects gathered for a communal meal. First held by the Christian communities of the 1st century A.D. they were revived by the Methodists in the 18th century for their quarterly meetings. Two-handled cups of tea were passed round and a Scripture Cake or a Caraway Seed Cake coloured with saffron was eaten.

Scripture Cake

Ingredients

		ch.	v.
4½ cupsful	1 Kings	4	22
1 ½ cupsful	Judges	5	25
2 cupsful	Jeremiah	6	26
2 cupsful	1 Samuel	30	12
2 cupsful	Nahum	3	12
1 cupful	Numbers	17	8
2 tablespoons	1 Samuel	14	25
Season to taste	11 Chronicles	9	9
1 pinch of	Leviticus	2	13
6 of	Jeremiah	17	11
½ cupful	Judges	4	19
2 teaspoons	Amos	4	5

Method

Follow Solomon's prescription for making a good boy (Proverbs 23 v. 14) and you will have a good cake.

Caraway Seed Cake

Ingredients

- 6 oz butter
- 6 oz sugar
- 8 oz self-raising flour
- 3 eggs
- Pinch of salt
- ¼ teaspoonful saffron
- Milk
- 2 teaspoonfuls caraway seeds

Method

Cream fat and sugar and add beaten eggs gradually. Melt saffron in milk. Add the flour, caraway seeds and salt to mix. Bake at Gas 4 (350°F) for 1½ hours.

Whether it is pure coincidence or part of the same tradition, I do not know, but the only place I have ever eaten Caraway Seed Cake is at chapel anniversaries when I was a child. I well remember the hard, yellow slabs of cake with sharp crescent-shaped seeds. It was not popular and we only ate it if nothing else was left. Chapel anniversaries (usually held on a Bank Holiday) were an opportunity for scattered members of a small sect to meet and hear a well-known preacher. Equally important, it was an occasion for the younger members to meet and (hopefully) find life-partners.

August 9th is the Feast of St Oswald, King of Northumbria, who was killed in the 7th century. On the Saturday nearest to St Oswald's Day the children of Grasmere carry new rushes to the church and are given gingerbread (see July for recipes).

August 12th is the Feast of St Clare of Assisi who founded the austere order of Poor Clares in the 13th century.

It also marks the beginning of the grouse-shooting season. Most recipes for grouse include an interesting relic of medieval cooking. Before plates were considered necessary, trenchers of four-day old bread were placed on the table and the dinner served on to it. The trencher soaked up any excess gravy and meat juices and rich people gave them away as alms. Poor people would have eaten them as part of the meal. According to Mrs Beeton, grouse, ortolan, partridge, pigeon, ptarmigan, snipe and woodcock should still be served on a piece of fried bread or toast.

Roast Grouse

Ingredients

- A brace of grouse
- 2 oz butter
- 2 rashers of bacon
- Flour
- Seasoning
- 2 rounds of fried bread

Method

Place a piece of butter inside the birds and cover the breast with strips of bacon. Roast at Gas 6 (400°F) for 30-40 minutes basting occasionally. At the end of cooking remove the bacon, dredge with flour and baste well. Return to the oven placed on the fried bread to soak up meat juices. Leave for 10 minutes, then serve up hot with bread sauce.

Grouse Soup

Ingredients

- Grouse
- ½ pint red wine
- 2 pints stock
- 2 sticks celery
- 2 tablespoonfuls oatmeal
- Seasoning

Method

Roast a brace of grouse and dice the flesh. Put the carcasses in a large pan with celery, stock and seasoning and simmer for two hours. Strain. Add diced grouse, oatmeal and red wine and simmer for 30 minutes.

August 15th is the Feast of the Assumption of the Virgin Mary and herbs picked on that day are believed to have the greatest power of healing.

August 24th is the Feast of St Bartholomew, one of the 12 apostles.

Legend says that he was martyred by being flayed alive and his emblem in art is a butcher's knife. At Croyland Abbey little knives were given to visitors on St Bartholomew's Day. A favourite dish for this day was Barthelmas Beef.

Barthelmas Beef

METHOD

Soak brisket of beef for 24 hours in white wine. Drain the meat and sift over it a mixture of cinnamon, nutmeg, ginger and cloves. Place it in an earthenware pot and cover it with water. Seal the top well with foil and bake in a slow oven until very tender. It can be served hot or cold.

St Bartholomew is the patron saint of Bee-keepers. There are many superstitions and legends concerning bees, probably because bees were so important years ago. In Anglo-Saxon times they provided the only means of sweetening food. Beeswax candles were used to give light, and the only fermented drinks available were mead, metheglin and honey beer. Later, wines were introduced and imported under the Normans and other forms of lighting were invented, but it was not until the 18th century that sugar superseded honey as the main sweetening agent.

From early times, bees have been regarded as sacred, and to kill one is still considered unlucky in some places. Plato thought that the souls of sober people came to life again as bees, while Mahomet said that bees were admitted as souls to Paradise.

In Christian times they have been regarded as the divine and foretellers of the future. They were messengers of God as they were privileged to make wax for altar candles. Their humming was interpreted as anthems of praise and in some places people say that on Christmas Eve the bees in their hives hum the Hundredth Psalm.

Considering how highly bees were regarded it is not surprising that so many superstitions surround them. In some places the fishermen chase the first bee that they see in April. If they catch it they believe that they will have a good herring season. In Ireland there is an old legend of how a chief waging war on another clan asked the assistance of Gabriel who obligingly turned all the bees in his hives into spearmen enabling him to triumph over his enemy.

One of the most widely known superstitions is 'telling the bees' which is still practised in some country districts. Another is the fear that if a swarm settles on a dead bush or tree there will be a death in the family. Both these superstitions are illustrated in Mary Webb's novel *Precious Bane*.

Bees were told of any births, marriages or deaths in the family. After telling of a death, silence was observed for a few minutes. Then, if the bees began to hum it was a sign that they were content to stay with the new owner. An invitation to the funeral would be pinned to the hive, together with a piece of black crepe, and as the corpse left the house the hive would be turned around sunwise. Afterwards some of the funeral cake and drink would be placed by the hive for the bees to feed on. If one omitted to do any of these things it was feared the bees would leave.

Another custom still in existence is 'tanging' the bees when they swarm. It was thought that if a swarm settled on someone else's land the owner could not claim them unless they had been followed making a loud clattering noise with a poker and shovel or some other noisy domestic implement. One could not be accused of trespassing whilst 'tanging' and the noise was said to make the bees settle more quickly and not fly too far afield.

The superstitions concerning bees may not all be nonsense. The ancients believed that the sting of a bee cured rheumatism, and that when no bees leave a hive, rain is imminent, and these may well be based on fact.

Honey is still regarded as a health-giving food as it is an easily digested form of energy. It gives a delicious flavour to biscuits, cakes and the popular medieval drink Metheglin.

Honey Shortbread

Ingredients

- 8 oz self-raising flour
- 4 oz butter
- 8 oz honey

Method

Work all the ingredients into a dough. Roll and cut into shapes and bake in slow oven.

Honey Biscuits

Ingredients

- 1 pound of honey
- 2 oz sugar
- 2 oz butter
- A pinch of ginger
- Flour

Method

Mix together the honey, sugar, butter and ginger and work in enough flour to make a stiff paste. Roll out thinly, cut into shapes and bake in a fast oven.

Metheglin

Ingredients

- 2 gallons water
- 4 pints of clear honey
- 3 lemons
- 2 lbs granulated sugar
- A few cloves
- 3 sprigs of rosemary
- 1 piece of root ginger
- 1 oz yeast (on a piece of toast)

Method

Boil the sugar and honey in the water and add the lemon juice and rind, cloves, ginger and rosemary. Cool to blood heat and add yeast. Leave until fermentation has ceased for about a week. Strain and bottle. Keep for nine months before drinking.

Because honey is antiseptic it was also used in many ointments and my favourite cough mixture when I was a child was a home-made one using honey, lemon juice and glycerine. Here is a recipe for a rather sticky ointment.

Chilblain Ointment

Ingredients

- 1 tablespoon honey
- 1 tablespoon glycerine
- White of an egg
- Flour

Method

Mix honey, glycerine and egg white together and add enough flour to make a paste. Spread over the chilblains and cover with a bandage.

September

"September blow soft
Till fruit be in loft."

September was the seventh month in the Roman Calendar, and although later January and February were added, the names of the last four months were never changed.

The Anglo-Saxons called it 'Gerst-monath' or Barley Month as this was the month for the barley harvest.

September 1st

"Fair on First of September,
Fair for a month."

St Giles' Day falls on September 1st. He is the patron saint of cripples and his emblem in art is an arrow. On St Giles' Day people were allowed to eat Mayne Bread which, in the Middle Ages, was only made on Whitsunday, St Giles' Day, Yule and Pasch (Easter). In York, Mayne bread was presented to important visitors to the city on St Giles' Day.

York Mayne Bread

Ingredients

- 12 oz plain flour
- 8 oz sugar
- 3 egg yolks
- 2 egg whites
- Teaspoonful coriander seed
- Teaspoonful caraway seed
- 2 teaspoonfuls rose water
- ½ oz yeast
- A little warm milk

Method

Mix yeast in warm water. Beat the egg whites until stiff. Add the egg yolks to the rose-water. Mix the flour, sugar, coriander and caraway seeds. Add all the other ingredients and leave to rise for 20 minutes. Roll out and shape and rise again. Bake in a moderate oven until golden brown.

There were many different kinds of bread in Elizabethan times. The finest which was only eaten by the rich was called manchet and was made from wheat. Poor people ate barley or rye bread. Now everyone eats wheaten bread, but at one time bread was made from whichever cereal grew best locally. In Norfolk and Suffolk bread was made from rye; in Wales and Cornwall from barley and in Scotland from oats. When cereals were short, peas, beans and even acorns were ground to make rather inferior bread. Nowadays brown bread is becoming more popular and dieticians tell us that it is better for our health than over-refined white bread, but when only rich people could afford white bread, brown bread was despised. There was a popular saying 'It is a good thing to eat your brown bread first' meaning that it is best to get misfortunes and poverty over early in life.

Oatmeal bread is very dry but it has the advantage of keeping good for a long time. In Scotland oatmeal was made into Riddle Bread.

Riddle Bread

Method

Mix yeast with warm water and add enough oatmeal to make a thick porridge. Leave overnight in a warm room. Salt to taste and then spread the mixture on the bakestone and brown on one side. Hang it from the ceiling and use when needed.

There are many other recipes for different kinds of bread but these two, York Mayne and Riddle Bread, which both date from the Middle Ages, are good examples of the difference between the bread eaten by rich and poor people.

A good many bakers were rogues who thought nothing of adulterating the flour with chalk to make the bread look whiter and the Assize of Bread was introduced to lay down standards and legislate against offenders.

William Cobbett, writing in 1821, had very strong opinions on the value of home-baked bread and urged housewives to go back to baking their own bread and brewing beer – the foods that made England great. He had a theory that the evils of poverty were largely due to eating potatoes and drinking tea. He described tea as 'a destroyer of health, an enfeebler of the frame, an engenderer of effeminacy and laziness, a debaucher of youth and a maker of misery for old age' and he deplored the time wasted with the 'clattering tea-tackle'.

On potatoes (which he called 'Ireland's lazy root') his language was even stronger. He says:

"How many fires; what a slopping and what a messing. The cottage everlastingly in a litter; the woman's hand everlastingly wet and dirty; the children grimed up to the eyes with dust fixed on by potato starch; and ragged as colts. The poor mother's time all being devoted to the everlasting boiling of the pot."

A rather extravagant way to describe cooking potatoes! Potatoes were a staple food in Ireland long before they were popular in the rest of Britain and were often eaten with sugar and milk. If you would like to try a sweet recipe using potatoes, here is a Potato Souffle.

Potato Souffle

Ingredients

- 1 pound potatoes (cooked and mashed)
- 3 oz butter
- 4 eggs
- 2 oz sugar
- 2 oz flaked almonds
- 3 tablespoonfuls sherry
- 2 tablespoonfuls flour
- Orange essence
- Nutmeg
- Salt

Method

Stir butter, sugar and seasonings into potato. Add beaten eggs. Mix the flour with the sherry and orange essence and add to mixture. Stir in the almonds. Bake at Gas 4 (350°F) for 45 minutes.

The Wednesday, Friday and Saturday after 14th September are Ember Days. The other Ember Days are the Wednesday, Friday and Saturday following the first Sunday in Lent, the Feast of Pentecost and December 13th. They are a relic of the time when *all* Wednesdays, Fridays and Saturdays were fast days.

'The Forme of Cury', a recipe book dated 1378, gives a special Ember Day Onion Tart which complies with the church edict to regard these days as days of abstinence.

Ember Day Onion Tart

Ingredients

- 12 oz flour
- 6 oz lard
- 4 oz sliced onions
- 1 oz butter
- 3 eggs
- ½ pint milk
- ½ cup breadcrumbs
- 4 oz mixed fruit
- Pinch of cinnamon
- Salt and pepper

Method

Make pastry with flour, lard and water and bake blind in a flan case for 15 minutes. Fry the sliced onions in butter and put in flan case. Beat eggs with milk and add breadcrumbs, fruit and seasoning. Pour over onions and bake for 30 minutes at Gas 3 (335°F).

September 18th is the anniversary of the birth of Dr Samuel Johnson at Lichfield in 1709. A candlelit supper is held each year in his honour. It is not really an old British custom but I am including it to give his admirers a good excuse to enjoy his favourite meal of Steak and Kidney Pudding with Mushrooms, Apple Tart and Cream and Hot Punch.

Steak and Kidney Pudding with Mushrooms

Ingredients

For suet crust:

- 6 oz self-raising flour
- 3 oz shredded suet
- Pinch of salt

For the filling:

- 1 pound stewing steak
- 1 sheep's (or 3 oz ox) kidney
- ¼ pound mushrooms
- 1 dessertspoonful flour
- Stock
- Seasoning

Method

Line a bowl with two-thirds of the pastry. Cut meat and kidney into small pieces and toss in seasoned flour. Mix with mushrooms and put into basin. Add a little stock and cover with the rest of the pastry. Cover with a floured cloth or foil and steam for five hours. Thicken the rest of the stock and serve separately.

Apple Tart

Ingredients

- 8 oz flour
- 4 oz butter
- 2 pounds of apples
- 4 oz sugar
- Grated lemon rind

Method

Make pastry with flour and butter and use half to line an 8 inch plate. Place half the peeled and sliced apples on the pastry and sprinkle with the sugar. Add the remaining apple slices and cover with the rest of the pastry, sealing the edges well with a little water. Bake at Gas 6 (400°F) for 40 minutes and then reduce the heat for a further 20 minutes to cook the apples. Dredge with castor sugar and serve with cream.

Hot Punch

INGREDIENTS

- ½ pint rum
- ½ pint brandy
- 1 pint boiling water
- 1 lemon
- 3 oz sugar
- Pinch each of cinnamon, nutmeg, cloves

METHOD

Remove the zest of the lemon and extract the juice. Put all ingredients in a large saucepan and heat gently. Do not allow it to boil. Serve in a large punch bowl.

A cheaper version can be made by adding a quart of ale.

September 21st is St Matthew's Day. He was the tax-collector who wrote the first of the Gospels and his symbol is a man with wings.

September 28th is the Feast of St Wenceslas, a Bohemian prince, who is remembered in the Christmas carol 'Good King Wenceslas'.

September 29th is dedicated to St Michael and All Angels (Michaelmas Day). It is one of four quarter days. The others are Lady Day (25th March), Midsummer Day (24th June) and Christmas Day (25th December). The quarter days in Scotland fall on Candlemas (February 2nd), Whitsunday (15th May or nearest Sunday), Lammas (1st August) and Martinmas (11th November).

Servants would be hired for a period of years or months ending on a quarter day so it was a convenient day to hold hiring fairs. These are described in many books such as Mary Webb's *Precious Bane* and Thomas Hardy's *Tess of the D'Urbervilles*. The young men and women seeking employment would carry a tool of their trade so that farmers looking for employees, or people needing servants, could easily identity them.

Dairymaids carried a stool, shepherds a crook, cowmen a pail and gardeners a spade. A cook would carry a wooden spoon and a housemaid a broom.

Servants often terminated their employment on the Christmas quarter day and took a new post from New Year's Day to ensure a short holiday with their families at Christmas time. A practice which must have been most inconvenient for their employers.

In some places servants only commenced a new job on weekdays as it was said that

"Saturday servants never stay
Sunday servants run away."

The hiring fairs must have been exciting for children, with 'quack' doctors selling patent remedies, dentists extracting teeth and stalls selling 'fairings' for them to take home. Traditional fairings included gingerbread (see July for recipes), brandy snaps and toffee apples.

Brandy Snaps

Ingredients

- ½ pound syrup
- ¼ pound flour
- 4 oz moist brown sugar
- 4 oz butter
- ½ teaspoonful ground ginger
- Rind and juice of a lemon
- 1 tablespoonful brandy

Method

Melt the sugar, butter and syrup in a pan and stir in the flour, ginger, brandy and lemon. Mix well and drop in small teaspoonfuls on a greased baking sheet leaving plenty of room for them to spread. Bake at Gas 3 (330°F) for about 10 minutes. As soon as they are cool enough, wrap them round the handle of a wooden spoon and leave to set.

Toffee Apples

Ingredients

- 12 apples
- 1 pound sugar
- 4 oz butter
- 2 tablespoonfuls water

Method

Put a clean stick of wood firmly into each apple. Melt sugar, butter and water in a saucepan and then boil to 290°F. Dip apples into cold water then into the toffee and back again into cold water. Drain on waxed paper.

The traditional meal for Michaelmas is goose and there is a saying that if you eat goose on Michaelmas Day you will not want for money during the coming year. When geese were driven to market they were first made to walk through tar and then sand and this formed 'shoes' which protected their feet.

A lady from Whitby wrote telling me "people always came to dinner on Michaelmas Sunday to have roast Michaelmas goose. This was a young goose that had been fattened on the harvest stubble. On a fine day in Autumn the farmer's wife would go for a couple of hours into the fields with the geese and while they ate, she would gather brambles".

Tradition says that on Michaelmas Day the devil fell into a bramble patch and cursed it and this is the latest day to gather blackberries. It is also the date for the apple harvest and in Somerset the little apples are left on the trees for the pixies. So the traditional meal for Michaelmas is Roast Goose, Blackberry and Apple Pie and Michaelmas Cake.

Roast Goose

Ingredients

- 1 goose
- Fat for basting
- Flour
- 4 oz breadcrumbs
- 1 teaspoonful dried sage
- ½ pound onions
- 1 egg
- 2 oz butter
- Salt and pepper

Method

Slice the onions and boil them in a little water for a few minutes. Mix with sage, breadcrumbs, butter, egg and seasoning and use to stuff the goose. Prick the bird well all over with a fork and roast at Gas 6 (400°F) for 2 ½ hours. Dredge flour over breast, baste and cook for 15 minutes. Serve with apple sauce.

Blackberry and Apple Pie

Ingredients

- 6 oz flour
- 3 oz butter
- 1½ pounds apples
- ½ pound blackberries
- 4 oz sugar

Method

Make shortcrust pastry using flour, butter and a little water. Peel and slice the apples and put apples, blackberries and sugar in a pie dish in layers, finishing with apples. Cover with pastry and bake at Gas 6 (400°F) for 40 minutes, then reduce heat for a further 15 minutes.

Michaelmas Cake

Method

Put equal quantities of oats, barley and rye in a bowl with a little melted butter and enough water to form a dough. Roll into a flat cake and bake. During baking baste with a batter made of oatmeal, eggs, butter and milk so that it forms several layers.

At Michaelmas, the pig which had roamed free and eaten on common land during the summer was caught (before someone else caught it) to be fattened up for killing at Martinmas in November.

"At Michaelmas safely go sty up they boar
Lest straying abroad ye do see him no more."

October

“Then came October
Full of merry glee…”

October, like September, November and December, is mis-named, as it has not been the eighth month since Roman times. The Saxons called it ‘Winter-fullith’ as this month marked the onset of winter.

October 12th is St Wilfrid’s Day. St Wilfrid is the patron saint of Ripon and when his feast is celebrated jam and lemon tarts are placed in dishes outside people’s houses for passers-by to help themselves. (The correspondent who sent me the recipe told me that nowadays this celebration takes place on August Bank Holiday and not on the saint’s feast day.)

At one time every town and village celebrated its own ‘Feast Day’, which was the date of the patron saint of their parish church. The celebration of the anniversaries of the saints goes back to the middle of the 2nd century A.D. The early church encouraged the remembrance of the first Christian martyrs as an inspiration to the faithful in times of persecution, when their heroism was held up as an example to the faint-hearted. On feast days special prayers were said and lessons read and after Mass the day would be given over to feasting, games, a pageant or a fair. Many towns still have a ‘Feast Field’ where a fair still comes each year to coincide with the patronal festival of the parish church. Until quite recently, relatives would try to meet on Feast Day and there are a number of regional dishes which became the traditional food for these occasions.

Wilfra Tarts

Ingredients

- 8 oz flour
- 4 oz butter
- ¼ lb raspberry jam
- 1 pint milk
- 1 dessertspoonful vinegar
- 1 egg
- 1 oz sugar
- 1 oz sultanas
- 1 oz currants

Method

Make pastry with the flour and butter and put into patty tins. Fill half of them with raspberry jam. Warm the milk to blood heat and add the vinegar. When it is cool add the egg, sugar and fruit and use this mixture to fill the rest of the tins. Bake at Gas 7 (425°F) for 10 minutes.

October 18th is St Luke's Day. St Luke the evangelist was a doctor and is the patron saint of physicians and surgeons.

> "On St. Luke's Day
> The oxen get leave to play."

as St Luke's symbol in art is an ox.

In Scotland they eat Sour Cakes on St Luke's Day. The recipe is very old and is believed to have a pagan origin.

St. Luke's Sour Cakes

METHOD

Mix oatmeal, sugar, water and a little cinnamon to make a dough. Leave in a bowl for a week to 10 days then roll out into small cakes (as thinly as possible). Bake until crisp.

This recipe is very similar to one I have come across which was used by American pioneering families in the 19th century. They used cornmeal which they allowed to ferment for several days before making their biscuits. Housewives would keep a jar of flour and warm water on a shelf by the stove to make 'sour dough'. Some of it would be added to fresh cornmeal, salt and water to make the biscuits. After making them the scraps were put back in the jar with more warm water. Some of the sour dough was always left in the jar to help work the next batch of biscuit scraps (rather like making yoghurt).

October 25th is the Feast of St Crispin and St Crispinian, martyrs and the patron saints of shoe-workers. Their emblems are a shoe or a last.

October 28th is the Feast of St Simon and St Jude and marked the end of the fishing season.

"On Simon and Jude
The ships home do crowd."

At Wellingborough (where I used to live) the patronal festival in October was celebrated with the local speciality 'Hock and Dough', which was usually cooked in the baker's oven to be collected after the church service. Hock and Dough is a great favourite with my family and is a typical regional dish in that there is no recipe. I was raised on it and thought I knew exactly how it should be made, but there being some dispute as to what constituted the genuine, original dish, I visited a Wellingborough pensioners' club to find out if any of the members could tell me how to make it. After asking a dozen ladies (and getting as many recipes) one fact emerged. Basically it is an open pie cooked in a large meat tin with pastry round the outside and meat, vegetables and gravy in the centre. The choice of meat used probably depended upon a family's personal preference or income. Some use hock of pork (which sounds logical) while others use pig's fry, liver, heart, belly of pork, trotters or pork cuttings, though it is agreed that some form of pig's meat should be used. The pastry can be either shortcrust or suet crust and can either be used just to line the edges of the tin or can cover the bottom as well.

Hock and Dough

Ingredients

- 12 oz pastry
- A hock of pork
- 2 pounds potatoes
- 1 pound onions
- 1 pound carrots
- 1 pint of stock
- Seasoning

Method

Place the pastry round the edges of the meat tin. Place the meat in the centre and surround it with vegetables. Pour the stock and seasoning over it and bake in a moderate oven for one and a half hours.

One reason why this dish was so popular in the past is that it was a very convenient one to carry to the bakehouse in the days when few homes owned an oven. The complete dinner being cooked in one dish made it easier to transport. Bakehouse cooking was continued locally on a large scale until about the Second World War and some bakers still cook Christmas turkeys. When I was a child my teachers (two elderly sisters) would carry their meat in a tin to the bakehouse before school, with a jug containing batter to pour round it towards the end of cooking. Local bakers have told me that at one time there was a bakehouse on practically every street corner and they regularly cooked 30 to 40 meals, including pies and tarts, as the ovens were still hot for several hours after the bread was removed. Sometimes housewives would bring them a basin of dried fruit, sugar and spices which they would then add to a piece of bread to make a Feast Monday Dough Cake. This is also described in Flora Thompson's wonderful account of rural life *Lark Rise to Candleford*. There are fewer local bakers nowadays so here is a recipe a lady sent me for Feast Monday Dough Cake.

Feast Monday Dough Cake

INGREDIENTS

- 8 oz plain flour
- 4 oz butter
- 6 oz sugar
- 6 oz mixed fruit
- 1 teaspoonful mixed spice
- ½ pint milk
- Pinch of salt
- ½ oz yeast

Method

Cream the yeast with a teaspoonful of sugar and mix with tepid milk. Sift flour, spice and salt and rub in butter. Add sugar and fruit. Add yeast mixture and knead well. Place in a loaf tin and leave in a warm place for one hour. Bake at Gas 6 (400°F) for one hour.

October 31st is Halloe'en, the Eve of the Feast of All Hallows, once the Festival of Samhain. In Cornwall it is called Allantide, and Allan apples were given for luck. One kept under the pillow was supposed to encourage dreams of one's future husband.

At Halloe'en, boys were given an opportunity to dream of their future wife – the only instance I have found; usually girls did the dreaming. They would gather 10 leaves of ivy without speaking, throw one away and put the others under their pillow to induce dreams of their loved one.

Halloe'en is steeped in pagan superstition and rituals which are still carried out, especially north of the border. There were two main seasons in the Celtic year. Beltane (The Festival of Summer) and Samhain (the Festival of Winter) which marked the beginning of the year in Anglo-Saxon times.

Halloe'en has always been associated with the idea of death. Death of the vegetation and death of the livestock which was killed at the beginning of winter and smoked or salted to save having to feed the animals through the winter months.

The last sheaf of corn was left until Samhain and then cut and dressed as a female figure called the Maiden. This represented the Spirit of the Corn and was hung on the wall until the next ploughing time when it was broken up and ploughed into the land. The figures gradually became more stylized until they turned into the 'Corn Dollies' which we still see today in craft shops or country cottages.

Samhain is an example of a pagan festival which has been Christianized. In 998, Odilo, Abbot of Cluny, ordained a Mass for the souls of the dead to be held on what we now call All Saints' Day. Far from ridding this season of superstition, it appears to have had the effect of adding a few more.

In Ireland people believe that the souls in purgatory are released for forty-eight hours when they re-visit their old homes. Food is left out for them, rooms are left unswept in case a soul is unwittingly swept out, and all water is covered so that souls cannot fall in and drown.

In some places warm pancakes, curds and cider were put out as a 'feast for the dead'. Journeys were avoided and necessary ones only undertaken after filling the pockets with salt.

At Samhain the cows which had not been killed were brought into the cowsheds for the winter and rowan (or mountain ash) was tied to the cowshed door to prevent the witches from suckling the cows' milk.

The witches received the blame for most domestic calamities. If the bread failed to rise because the yeast was not prepared properly, or if the butter in the churn would not solidify, housewives found it convenient to believe that it was the work of witches. Murrain in cattle, disease in the crops, or the birth of a deformed child, could all be explained in this way. Defenceless and eccentric old countrywomen who had outlived their families led a precarious existence if too many disasters overtook a community. Perhaps sometimes it worked the other way around and some women played on ignorant people's fears for their own protection.

Halloe'en was another Fire Festival, when the Druids lit bonfires in thanks to the Sun-God for the harvest.

There are many recipes connected with Halloe'en. The following is for a drink known as Lambswool, which is believed by some to be a corruption of Lamasbhal – the spirit which presides over fruit and seeds.

Lambswool

Ingredients

- 2 pints of ale
- 4 eggs
- 1 pound roasted apples
- 6 oz sugar
- Beaten egg
- Pinch of nutmeg, cloves, ginger

Method

Simmer the ale and gradually stir in the beaten egg. Add the rest of the ingredients and serve very hot.

Buttered Sowans was a popular Halloe'en dish in Scotland. A ring was concealed in it and the finder could expect to be married within a year.

Buttered Sowans

Ingredients

- 8 oz oatmeal sids (inner husk of oats)
- Twice the volume of water
- Salt
- Butter
- Cream
- Whisky

Method

Put the oatmeal sids in an earthen pot and cover with the water. Leave for ten days and then sieve and discard the sids. Leave for another three days to settle and then carefully pour off the thin liquid. The sediment that is left is the 'sowans'. Heat it until it is thick and beat a little butter into it. Lace it well with whisky and serve hot with cream.

Another favourite at Halloe'en is the Dough Cake. It is called different things in different places. In Scotland they call it Selkirk Bannock, in Ireland Barm Brack and in Wales Bara Brith or Speckled Bread.

Halloe'en Dough Cake

Ingredients

- 2 pounds of dough from the bakehouse
- 12 oz butter
- 8 oz sugar
- 2 pounds sultanas

Method

Rub the butter into the dough and add the rest of the ingredients. Place in a tin and leave to rise for half an hour. Bake for 1¼ hours in a moderate oven.

Other Halloe'en dishes in Scotland are Cream Crowdie (see August), Champit Tatties (mashed potatoes) and Cloutie Dumpling which is a suet pudding with sultanas added. This is another dish with many names. We always called it Spotted Dick; if the sultanas are soaked un rum first it is known as Rum Dog and I understand that at girls' boarding schools it rejoices in the name of Matron's Leg.

Cloutie Dumpling

Ingredients

- 6 oz self-raising flour
- 3 oz shredded suet
- 4 oz sultanas
- 2 oz sugar
- Milk

METHOD

Mix all the ingredients together to make a soft dough. Form into a 'sausage' and boil for three hours in a floured pudding cloth. Serve with custard.

Irish recipes for Halloe'en include Colcannon, Potato apple cake and and Boxty Bread – all based on potatoes.

INGREDIENTS

- Mashed potatoes
- Well-chopped cooked cabbage
- Bacon fat
- Seasoning

METHOD

Mash the potaties with cabbage, seasoning and bacon fat. Fry over a low heat. Make a well in the top of each serving and fill with a knob of butter. It should be eaten by dipping forkfuls into the melted butter. (This is equally good with left-over brussels sprouts.)

Potato Apple Cake

Ingredients

- 2 pounds potatoes
- 1 pound apples
- 1 cup flour
- 2 oz butter
- 1 tablespoon white sugar
- 4 oz brown sugar
- ¼ teaspoonful ginger

Method

Cook and mash the potatoes and add the white sugar and half the butter. Blend in the flour and ginger. Divide the dough into two circles on the plate and cover with apple slices. Place the other circle on top. Bake for 30 minutes at Gas 6 (425°F). Remove the lid carefully and dot with the rest of the butter. Sprinkle with brown sugar and replace lid. Bake for another five minutes and serve hot.

Boxty Bread

Ingredients

- 2 pounds of potatoes
- Flour
- Salt

Method

Cook and mash two-thirds of the potatoes. Grate the other third raw and add to the mashed potatoes with a pinch of salt and enough flour to form a dough. Roll out and cut into rounds. Bake on a hot griddle and serve buttered.

Nowadays Halloe'en is celebrated with parties when the accent is on the mysterious and 'spooky'. Fortunes are told and games such as Bobbing for Apples are played.

The origins of these games go back to Celtic times when the divinations were taken much more seriously.

November

"At Hallomass, slaughter
time soon cometh in
And then doth the
husbandman's
feasting begin."

November, the ninth month in the Roman calendar was known as 'Wint-monath' or wind-month by the Saxons and marked the end of the fishing season.

"November take flail,
Let ship no more sail."

Threshing now takes place at the same time as harvesting because we have machinery which can do both operations at once, but years ago this must have been long and back-breaking work. For centuries it was done with a flail, but even after threshing machines arrived on the scene it was far from easy. In *Tess of the d'Urbervilles* Hardy describes the threshing of the last wheat-rick on a March morning with a chain of workers untying sheaves and feeding the machine which 'kept up a despotic demand upon the endurance of their muscles and nerves'.

November was also called 'Blot-monath' or Blood Month as it was the season when cattle were slaughtered and some of the animals sacrificed to the gods. Killing in Autumn continued until the late middle ages. The offal and blood was eaten fresh and the rest of the animal smoked or salted for the coming winter.

November 1st and 2nd are All Saints' Day and All Souls' Day. As mentioned in the preceding chapter, they coincide with a Celtic Festival for the dead.

A Mumming-play was held in Cheshire on All Souls' Day called the 'Soul-Caking-Play'.

Souling Cake

Ingredients

- 12 oz flour
- 6 oz butter
- 1 egg
- 1½ teaspoonful vinegar
- ½ teaspoonful cinnamon
- ½ teaspoonful mixed spice
- 6 oz sugar

Mix the dry ingredients together. Rub in the fat and beat in the egg and vinegar. Knead until soft. Roll out and cut into rounds and bake for 20 minutes at Gas 4 (350°F).

Soul cakes were given to callers who were then asked to pray for dead relatives and children would go 'a-souling' begging for soul cakes and singing a traditional souling song.

"A soul, a soul, a soul cake,
O Good Mistress, a soul cake,
An apple, a pear, a plum or a cherry,
Any good thing to make us merry,
One for Peter, one for Paul,
And one for Him who made us all."

Throughout the year there were a number of days when one could legitimately beg. Sometimes it was for money. Sometimes for cakes, apples, ale, clothes or even a holiday from school.

Two of the begging days have survived. Nowadays children bring a Guy round on 5th November begging for firework money, and later (but not much) they are back again singing carols.

The traditional 'begging songs' usually had something in common. There was nearly always a verse designed to make the listener feel guilty because he was warmer, better dressed or better fed than the singers outside. Whether the songs were written in this way in order to extort more money, or whether these happen to be the ones that are remembered as being the most successful, I do not know.

The Souling Song continues

"The lanes are very muddy,
Our shoes are very thin.
I've got a little pocket
To put a penny in."

A Leicestershire May Day Song says

"We have been travelling all the night
And the best part of the day
And now we have returned again
And have brought you a bunch of may."

A Wassail Song has the verse

"Good Master and Good Mistress
While you're sitting by the fire,
Pray think of us poor children
Who are wandering in the mire."

All guaranteed to rend the heartstrings!

November 5th is Guy Fawkes Night. Long before Guy Fawkes' time, November was a time for bonfires, mostly connected with Samhain. Now children burn a 'Guy' to celebrate the unsuccessful Gunpowder Plot when Guy Fawkes attempted to blow up Parliament in 1605. The children used to sing:

"Please to remember the fifth of November,
Gunpowder, treason and plot;
I see no reason why gunpowder treason
Should ever be forgot."

and

"Guy, guy, guy,
Stick him up on high,
Put him on the bonfire
And there let him die!"

Traditional treats for bonfire night are Tom Trot (a treacle toffee) and Parkin (a kind of gingerbread). This recipe for Guy Fawkes Parkin was sent to me from Yorkshire.

Guy Fawkes Parkin

Ingredients

- 6 oz flour
- 3 oz brown sugar
- 3 oz margarine or butter
- 2 oz medium oatmeal
- 4 oz golden syrup
- 1 egg
- 1 teaspoonful ground ginger
- 1 teaspoonful bicarbonate of soda

Method

Sift together the dry ingredients. Melt the syrup and margarine in a saucepan and then mix with the dry ingredients. Add the egg and enough milk to make a soft consistency. Bake in a well-greased flat tin for one hour at Gas 3 (325°F).

Tom Trot

Ingredients

- 8 oz dark brown sugar
- 8 oz black treacle
- 2 oz butter

Method

Simmer all ingredients for 30 minutes. Pour on a greased slab and pull until clear.

November 11th – Martinmas – is the Feast of St Martin, Bishop of Tours, who died in 397 A.D. He was at one time a Roman soldier and pictures of him usually illustrate the legendary incident when he gave half of his cloak to a beggar.

In the Aran Islands no woman must spin or miller grind corn on St Martin's Day. They have a particularly grisly legend of how St Martin begged a widow for food and having none she boiled her child and gave it to the saint for supper. After he left she went to the cradle to mourn and the baby was sleeping unharmed.

In the Middle Ages Martinmas was known as the Feast of Sausages as this was a traditional time for pig killing. A popular dish for Martinmas was Mell Cake or Pig-killing Cake, which was eaten warm at a party on the evening the pig was killed.

Ingredients

- 8 oz self-raising flour
- 4 oz butter
- 2 oz sugar
- 3 oz currants or sultanas

For filling:

- Butter, sugar and grated nutmeg

Method

Make a pastry with flour, butter, sugar and currants and a little water. Roll into a round about eight inches across. Bake until brown and then split it open and spread with the butter, sugar and nutmeg.

Serve hot.

Pig-killing was a great occasion. It was done during the first two quarters of the moon so that the meat would not shrink in the pot. For farm labourers, who had been denying themselves beer for weeks in order to buy food to fatten the pig, it usually represented the only meat they would see all winter. The pig's fry would be eaten straight away. Hams and sides of bacon would be soaked in brine before being hung up to dry, and the intestines would be cleaned to use as sausage skins. The head was made into Collared Pig's Head, the liver into Faggots, and the Fry was often cooked and served with dumplings.

Even the blood was not wasted as it was the main ingredient for the popular Black Pudding.

Collared Pig's Head

Ingredients

- The head, feet and hocks of a pig
- Salt
- Saltpetre
- Pepper
- Sage (rubbed fine)
- Pinch of mace, cloves and nutmeg

Method

Put the meat in water for 24 hours then drain. Cover with water and add 1 pound of salt and 1 oz saltpetre. Leave for five days and then boil until meat comes away from the bones easily. Chop it finely and add seasoning, herbs and spices. Leave overnight in a basin with a seven pound weight on top. Turn it out and slice.

Ingredients

- 1 pound pig's liver
- 2 oz breadcrumbs
- 2 onions
- Sage
- 1 egg
- Salt and pepper
- 4 oz margarine

Method

Mince the liver and onions and add all the other ingredients. Mix well and put the mixture into a large, well-greased meat tin. Cover with foil and bake for 50 minutes at Gas 6 (400°F) removing the foil towards the end of cooking to brown the top. Serve cut into squares either hot or cold. (If you can get a pig's caul, roll the mixture into balls and cook each one wrapped in a piece of caul).

Pig's Fry and Dumplings (a recipe from Norfolk)

Ingredients

- 1 pound pig's fry
- 4 small onions

For the Dumplings

- 4 oz plain flour
- 1 teaspoonful baking powder
- ½ teaspoonful salt
- Cold water

Method

Place the pig's fry in a baking tin with a little water and the onions. Sprinkle with flour, salt and pepper. Bake at Gas 3 (335°F) for two hours. Turn and baste it occasionally. Mix the flour, baking powder, salt and water together to form a dough and roll into balls. Boil for 15 minutes in a fast boiling saucepan of stock. Drain and serve with the pig's try.

Black Pudding

Ingredients

- 1 quart of pig's blood
- ½ pound of oatmeal
- ½ pound of suet
- ½ pint of milk
- Pepper and salt

Method

Mix all the ingredients together well, pour into a saucepan and bring to the boil. Pour into a pie dish and leave it to set. Cut into slices and fry.

In Scotland where Black Puddings were very popular, it was not even necessary to wait for an animal to be killed. Evidently it was quite a common practice to 'bleed' cattle with a lancet and obtain enough blood for a pudding whenever necessary.

Although this may sound barbarous it was certainly practical and probably injured the cattle little more than 'blood-doning' does a human being. To peasants who could not afford meat, it provided a necessary form of protein. Far more barbarous methods were used by the rich to obtain luxury foods. Geese were nailed down and forcibly fed to enlarge their livers for pate de foie gras. Animals were beaten to death to tenderize the meat and there is even a recipe for cooking a live goose by plucking it and then making a fire all round it to prevent its escape. As soon as it was giddy and began to stumble it was considered ready to carve.

Old cookery books often sound rather brutal because they are full of 'smiting and hewing'. 'Take hares and hew them to gobbets'; 'ram chickens together and serve them broken'; 'grynd hym smal'; and 'smite them to pieces' are all typical instructions. In the days when housewives often had to kill the bird or animal before cooking it there was no place for the squeamish and although as a child I often watched my mother skinning, plucking and drawing rabbits and poultry I must admit that I prefer mine oven-ready.

Nowadays we are too faddy (or health-conscious) to eat tainted meat and we throw away anything that smells the slightest bit 'off'. Early cookery books give a number of recipes for making tainted meat edible by soaking it in vinegar and spices or wrapping it in a cloth and burying it for a week. It does not sound very appetising but was probably no worse than some of the meat soldiers ate. When in battle with no time for cooking, a steak would be placed under the horse's saddle and after half an hour's hard riding it was considered edible!

November 22nd is St Cecilia's Day. St Cecilia is the patron saint of musicians, and concerts are often held on this day in her honour. At Deddington, Oxfordshire, a Pudden Pie Fair is held on 22nd November.

Deddington Pudden Pies

Ingredients

- 1 pound of puff pastry
- 1 quart of milk
- 3 eggs
- 6 oz sugar
- 4 oz ground rice
- 4 oz currants
- 1 lemon

Line oven-proof saucers or shallow dishes with the pastry. Mix the ground rice with a little milk and add the beaten eggs. Boil the rest of the milk with sugar and the rind of the lemon. Add the rice mixture and keep stirring for 10 minutes. Add the currants and pour the mixture into the saucers, almost filling them. Bake in a moderate oven until set and eat hot or cold.

November 23rd is the Feast of St Clement, probably the 4th Pope. His emblem is an anchor, as legend says he was bound to an anchor and thrown into the Black Sea. He is the patron saint of blacksmiths.

November 25th is the Feast of St Catherine who died in 310 A.D. after being tortured on a spiked wheel. On St Clement's Day and St Catherine's Day children went 'Clementing and Catterning' singing

"Cattern and Clement come year by year,
Some of your apples and some of your beer."

Wheel-shaped Cattern Cakes were eaten hot with mulled ale in Somerset. At Ampthill, in Bedfordshire, St Catherine, the patron saint of spinners and lacemakers appears to have become confused with Queen Catherine of Aragon. The Queen lived at Ampthill after her divorce from King Henry VIII and did much to encourage lacemaking. Tradition says that when trade was bad she would burn her lace and order more. St Catherine's Day was a holiday for lacemakers and spinners. At Peterborough the little girls would stop their spinning, choose a Queen and go around the large houses begging for money and food. Girls in the lacemaking trade went from house to house singing traditional songs and receiving cattern cakes. At night they let off fireworks, and the Catherine wheel derives its name from the manner of the saint's death.

Cattern Cakes

Ingredients

- 2 pounds of dough
- 2 oz sugar
- 2 oz butter
- 1 egg
- A few caraway seeds

Method

Make a yeast dough (as for bread). Knead well with the butter, sugar, egg and caraway seeds. Leave in a warm place for two hours to rise. Place on a floured baking tin and bake in a moderate oven for two hours.

Like St Agnes, St Catherine was a virgin, yet girls used to look on her as a husband-bringer. In Dorset they said

"O, St Catherine lend me thine aid,
And grant I may never die an old maid."

The last Sunday before Advent is known in the Midlands as 'Stir-up Sunday'. The Collect for the day begins

"Stir up, we beseech Thee, O Lord, the hearts of
Thy faithful people."

and when housewives sitting in their pews heard these words they knew that it was time to make their Christmas puddings. Children visited houses and sang

"Stir up, we beseech thee
The pudding in the pot
And when we get home
We'll eat the lot."

(The recipes and history of the Christmas pudding are in the chapter on December.)

November 30th is St Andrew's Day or Anermas. St Andrew was a fisherman and Christ's first disciple. He is the patron saint of Scotland and his 'X'-shaped cross forms part of the Union Jack.

In Scotland a singed sheep's head boiled in Powsowdie (Barley Broth) and served with brain sauce was the traditional feast for Anermas.

Singed Sheep's Head

Method

Singe a sheep's head and boil gently for several hours until tender. Add carrots, turnips and onions to the water for the last hour. Remove the tongue and slice and serve the head split on a dish with the sliced tongue placed down the centre and surrounded by the vegetables.

Tree planting was always started in November as people believed that trees would only thrive if they were planted between All Hallows and Candlemas. Modern gardeners still choose this time to move trees and shrubs.

December

> "At Christmas play and make good cheer
> For Christmas comes but once a year.
> It brings us puddings, it brings us pies
> It brings us everything that's nice."

December was the tenth month in the Roman calendar and was named by the Saxons 'Winter-monath' or 'Midwinter'. At this season they held a feast called 'Giul' or 'Yule' dedicated to Thor, the god of Thunder. Several Yuletide customs are still observed in some form. The Druids used to choose a huge Yule Log which was blessed and then burned for twelve days of feasting. Afterwards the ashes would be burned in the fields and at the roots of fruit trees to make them fertile.

The Boar's Head, still traditionally eaten in some universities, dates back to a boar killed and sacrificed to the goddess Freya.

Miseltoe played an important part in Yuletide ceremonies. Because of its unusual parasitic growth it was considered magical and the Druids would cut it from the oak with a golden sickle.

December 6th is St Nicholas' Day. In many European countries St Nicholas (the original Santa Claus) is the traditiona1 'gift-bringer' and unlike Father Christmas he is a historical personage. St Nicholas was the Bishop of Myra and he liked to do good by stealth. The legend says that he heard of three sisters who were too poor to marry so he tossed three pieces of gold through the smoke-hole in their roof for a dowry. The gold fell into the stockings they had hung up to dry and this is why children still hang up a stocking at Christmas.

In Britain, Santa Claus and Father Christmas have merged into the same jolly personage, with red, fur-trimmed tunic and bushy eyebrows, but they have completely different origins. Early engravings of Father Christmas show a rather Bacchanalian figure crowned with vine leaves and carrying a wassail bowl. He appears to represent the spirit of the pagan Yule and perhaps his ancestry owes something to Odin, the Gift-bringer, who rode the sky during winter storms.

December 13th is St Lucy's Day. St Lucy, who is usually represented holding two eyes in a dish, is invoked against diseases of the eyes. The saying

"Lucy light, Lucy light
Shortest day and longest night."

suggests that some people thought that this was the shortest day.

December 21st is St Thomas Day. He was the Doubter who wanted positive proof of the Resurrection. As usual there is a saying,

"St Thomas gray, St Thomas
longest night and shortest day."

St Thomas's Day was considered the correct day to plant shallots which were supposed to be 'planted on the shortest day and pulled on the longest'. On St Thomas's Day poor women went 'a-Thomassing' when they would beg round the parish for corn for the Christmas cooking. The miller then ground it for them as his Christmas charity.

For some obscure reason St Thomas's Day was associated with onions. Some girls would place an onion under their pillow to induce dreams of their future husband. Others would take several onions and scratch on them the names of possible suitors. They then waited for them to sprout and the winner would be the girl's husband.

December 25th has been celebrated as the birthday of Jesus Christ since the 4th century. Earlier the day was sacred to Mithras, god of light.

The Christmas traditions are the ones we all know best because Christmas is the only one of the Church festivals that has popular appeal in Britain. From the Church's point of view it is not nearly as important as Easter and in many countries Easter is a far bigger celebration.

Sometimes people criticize the way we celebrate Christmas nowadays as if all the trimmings, evergreens, present-giving, candles and feasting have been added to the original simple Christmas of a church service and a bit of carol singing. They ignore the fact that Christmas was superimposed on to earlier festivals – the Celtic Yule, the Roman Saturnalia, etc., and that a holiday and feasting in the middle of Winter seems to have been a fundamental need, especially in countries with a long, dark winter.

For many years the playing of any kind of game was forbidden to the lower classes except during the 12 days of Christmas and a number of traditional Christmas games have a very long history. Blind Man's Buff is one of the oldest and Forfeits is another that goes back at least three hundred years. Snapdragon, which involves grabbing burning brandy-soaked raisins from a dish, is said to have originated as a Scandinavian initiation ritual, and the paper hats and balloons at parties are a remnant of the days when the Lord of Misrule presided over the festivities.

Most of the traditional Christmas food also has an extremely long history – in fact it is impossible in most cases to know how long. Mince pies were once called Shrid Pies and contained shredded meat and sometimes even fish. They were cooked in the shape of a manger with a pastry child in the lid. Later currants and spices were added and I have read that the spices were added after Crusaders brought them back from the Holy Land in the 13th century as people thought that the Lord's Nativity should be celebrated with something brought back from his birthplace. Actually, reading through medieval recipes one is struck by the lavish use of spices in most dishes, especially those containing meat, and I suspect that they may have been added for the practical reason of disguising the flavour of tainted meat.

During the Commonwealth mince-pies were banned, as the Puritans considered that, like so many things that were pleasant and enjoyable, they smacked of Popery. In fact, for eight years the Puritans succeeded in banning Christmas altogether. In 1652 they issued an Act which ran

> "No observation shall be had of the 25th day of December,
> commonly called Christmas Day;
> nor any solemnity used or exercised in churches
> upon that day in respect thereof."

Feasting was also forbidden, and until the Restoration in 1660 people worshipped in secret (and no doubt feasted in secret too). Eventually mince-pies returned, but now they were round tartlets and the pastry baby had disappeared. Some people try to eat 12 mince pies during the Christmas period as each one eaten is supposed to guarantee a happy month during the coming year.

Mince Pies

Ingredients

- ½ pound beef suet
- ½ pound apples
- ½ pound each raisins, sultanas, currants and mixed peel
- ½ pound brown sugar
- 1 teaspoonful mixed spice
- 2 oz ground almonds
- Rind and juice of a lemon
- Wineglass of brandy
- Shortcrust pastry

Method

Peel and mince the apples and put all the dried fruit through the mincer. Add the rest of the ingredients (except the pastry) and mix well together. Pack in jars and cover. This mincemeat will keep well for several months.

Roll out the pastry and use half to fill tartlet cases, reserving the rest for lids. Put a teaspoonful of mince-meat in each one, wet the edges and place the lids on top, pinching the edges well. Bake for 30 minutes at Gas 7 (430°F).

The Christmas Cake appears to have originated with the Twelfth Night Cake and the recipes are often almost identical. Some are richer than others and there are many recipes to choose from. I am including one that was passed down to me and is always very successful.

Christmas Cake

Ingredients

- ½ pound butter
- ½ pound castor sugar
- ½ pound plain flour
- ½ pound sultanas
- ½ pound currants
- ¼ pound glace cherries
- ¼ pound chopped whole almonds
- 6 oz mixed peel
- 5 eggs
- Rind and juice of a lemon
- 1 dessertspoonful raising powder
- 1 tablespoonful orange flower water
- 1 tablespoonful brandy
- Pinch of salt

Method

Cream the butter and sugar. Add the eggs and beat well. Add the dry ingredients, then the rind and juice of a lemon, orange flower water and brandy. Bake 1½ hours at Gas 2 (310°F) and then 2½ hours on Gas 1 (290°F) just below the centre of the oven in a tin lined with greaseproof paper.

To decorate: Brush the top with apricot glaze (made from warmed jam) and cover with a layer of marzipan. Leave for several days and then cover with icing and seasonal figures, wrapping a paper frill around the sides.

Originally Christmas cakes were not iced and the topping we now use – marzipan and icing sugar – comes from a popular medieval sweet known as a 'subtlety'. At some stage the two appear to have merged. A subtlety was made from marchpane (marzipan) moulded into fantastic shapes and then iced and gilded. Sometimes the design was chosen as a complement to the chief guest, such as a cathedral for a bishop, a castle for a baron or a ship for a merchant or explorer. The subtlety was brought on at the end of the meal (or at a large feast at the end of each course) and was intended to amaze and delight the guests.

The only parallel I can think of in modern cookery is the birthday cake. Many mothers spend the night before a child's birthday struggling to construct a representation of a spaceship or an engine with exactly the same aim.

Some subtleties were made with jellies and blancmange or an arrangement of fruit such as peaches and grapes would be set in jelly. A favourite was the 'Moon and Stars' which would make a very pretty dish for a party.

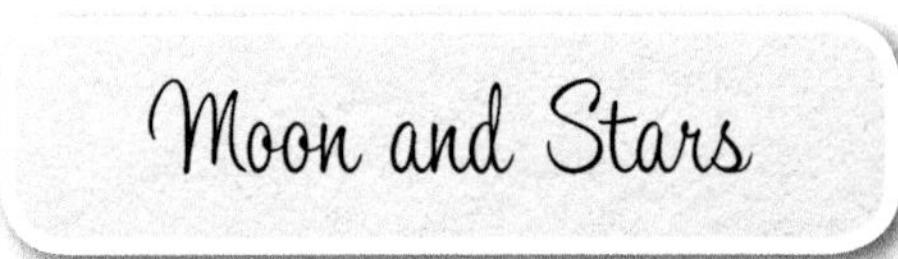

INGREDIENTS

- 2 orange jellies (made up with half the usual amount of water)
- 2 lemon jellies (made as directed)

METHOD

Make up the orange jellies and pour into star-shaped patty tins. Allow to set and turn out into a very large, round, shallow dish. Make up the lemon jellies and when almost cool pour over the 'stars'.

Many years ago, the traditional Christmas dinner for the very rich was a peacock. It would be skinned with the feathers and head intact and after cooking the skin would be put back on, the tail spread out and the beak painted gold. It was considered a great honour to be asked to carry it into the dining hall and this was usually done by the most beautiful lady present. Goose was popular until this century (and still is, in some households) but nowadays the favourite Christmas dinner is Roast Turkey. It is usually eaten with chipolata sausages, bread sauce, cranberry sauce, roast or mashed potatoes, brussels sprouts and giblet gravy. The turkey is stuffed with either parsley or chestnut stuffing and sometimes with sausagemeat as well. All the recipes are available in modern cookery books but these are some which were passed down to me.

Parsley Stuffing

Ingredients

- 1 pound white breadcrumbs
- ½ pound shredded suet
- ¼ pound chopped parsley
- 3 eggs
- Rind of 2 lemons
- Plenty of pepper and salt

Method

Mix all the ingredients well and pack loosely into the crop of the turkey. Sew the crop neatly.

Bread Sauce

Ingredients

- 2 oz white breadcrumbs
- ½ pint milk
- ½ oz butter
- 1 large onion
- 10 cloves
- Salt and pepper

Method

Peel the onion and stud it with cloves. Boil the milk, add the onion and leave it for an hour to infuse. Add the breadcrumbs and butter and reheat. Season to taste.

Years ago housewives always had a piece of Spiced Beef at Christmas and this would be an excellent choice for a buffet party nowadays as it could be served with a variety of salads.

Spiced Beef

Ingredients

- 3 pounds of salted beef
- 1 teaspoonful of salt
- 1 teaspoonful mixed spice
- 1 teaspoonful cinnamon
- 1 teaspoonful cloves
- 3 bay leaves
- 1 pint of cider

Method

Place the meat in a stewpot that is only slightly larger than the piece of meat. Cover it with the cider, spices and salt and leave for 12 hours. Remove meat and liquid to a larger pan and add enough water to cover the meat. Simmer for 3 hours. Serve cold.

A favourite cold dish for Christmas in Yorkshire was the famous Christmas Pie. These were made and sent up to London so they had to be sealed well with six pounds of butter to prevent them going bad. I must admit that I have not tried this recipe – it is far too expensive.

Christmas Pie

Method

> Bone a turkey, a goose, a chicken and a pigeon. Place the pigeon inside the chicken, then into the goose and then the turkey. Make a large pastry raised pie with very thick crust – reserving enough pastry for the lid. Place the turkey in the centre and fill up any spaces with small game birds (also boned). Pour over it six pounds of butter and seal with the lid.

I have not found any directions as to how long to cook it, but it would obviously take several hours. The idea is rather like an Egyptian recipe I came across which also consists of a number of birds and animals placed inside each other and eventually being sewn up inside a camel.

The oldest meat dish I have found for Christmas is Fat Brose which was evidently eaten by everyone in Scotland on Yule Day morning (according to Scott). It is a kind of stew with oatmeal dumplings.

Fat Brose

Method

Put half an ox head into a pan and cover with water. Boil until the fat is extracted and floating on top of the saucepan. Toast 2 oz of oatmeal with a pinch of salt, pour on a little of the hot fat and stir until it forms lumps. Put the lumps back into the pot to re-heat, stir the fat into the broth and serve.

Another old Scottish recipe is the Yule Bannock, a kind of shortbread with notched edges to represent the sun's rays – a relic of sun-worship.

Yule Bannock

Ingredients

- 8 oz flour
- 2 oz sugar
- 4 oz butter

Method

Place all the ingredients on a board and knead together until you have a firm dough. Press out into a circle and flute the edges with your fingers. Prick the top all over with a fork and bake at Gas 4 (380°F) until it begins to turn brown. Reduce the heat and finish cooking (about 1 hour altogether).

In Durham, bakers would make Yule Bread baked in the form of a baby to give to their regular customers at Christmas.

Yule Bread

Ingredients

- 3 pounds flour
- ½ pound sugar
- ½ pound currants
- ½ pound sultanas
- ¼ pound lard
- 2 oz margarine
- 2 oz lemon peel
- 1 dessertspoonful mixed spice
- 2 oz yeast
- Warm milk

Method

Mix the yeast in a little warm milk. Rub the fat into the flour and add the rest of the dry ingredients. Mix in the yeast mixture and enough warm milk to form a dough. Leave in tins to rise and bake in a moderate oven.

We usually finish our Christmas dinner with a Christmas pudding (if we have room). It has not always been the concoction we know now – steamed in a basin, or bought in a foil container. At one time it was known as Plum Pottage or Plum Porridge and was a much softer mixture served as an accompaniment to venison or poultry.

Plum Porridge

Ingredients

- 1 gallon of stock
- ½ pound sugar
- 1 pound raisins
- 1 pound currants
- l pint claret
- Breadcrumbs

Boil up the stock, claret and fruit with the sugar and add enough breadcrumbs to thicken. Simmer until well blended.

Later the porridge stiffened, the stock was left out and eggs added, and it became the Plum Pudding which was tied up in a cloth and boiled in a copper. In *A Christmas Carol* Dickens describes Mrs Cratchit entering

> "flushed, but smiling proudly – with the pudding,
> like a speckled cannon-ball, so hard and firm,
> blazing in half a quartern of ignited brandy,
> and bedight with Christmas holly stuck in the top."

Fortunately most Christmas cooking can not only be done in advance but actually improves with time. All the recipes containing a large amount of fruit – mince-meat, Christmas cake and Christmas Pudding – can be cooked at least a month before they are needed.

Christmas Pudding

Ingredients

- 8 oz sultanas
- 8 oz currants
- 4 oz raisins
- 4 oz mixed peel
- 12 oz breadcrumbs
- 6 oz suet
- 2 oz flour
- 8 oz soft brown sugar
- Rind of 2 lemons
- 2 teaspoonsful mixed spice
- 1 teaspoonful salt
- 4 eggs
- 1 tablespoonful black treacle
- Milk to mix (and a little brandy)

Method

Mix the flour and spices and add the suet, fruit and sugar. Beat the eggs and add them with enough milk to make a moist mixture. Add the brandy. Fill well-greased basins and cover with cloth or foil. Boil for seven hours, checking occasionally to make sure the saucepan does not boil dry. Store in a cool place. Boil for another 2 hours when required. Serve with cream, rum butter or rum sauce.

Some sources claim that the origin of the Christmas Pudding is Frumenty, one of the earliest known recipes in Britain and eaten in the north of England at Christmas time.

Frumenty (sometimes spelt Frummity or Furmenty) was a kind of porridge made with wheat which had been cooked for about two days until it was a stiff jelly. It sounds stodgy and unpalatable, and it probably was, because as the years went by, more and more ingredients were added to make it more interesting. First spices, and later currants, raisins and suet were added until it gradually evolved into the pudding we eat now.

But Frumenty in its original form has not been forgotten. In Yorkshire it is still eaten on Christmas Eve, and I have received many letters from North Country women telling me how to cook it and giving me details of local customs and traditions connected with it. Basically it is made as follows:

Frumenty

METHOD

> Put 8 oz of wheat into a large pie dish and fill with cold water. Put in a slow oven and cook (adding more water if required) until it has turned into a jelly. stir into warm milk and simmer until creamy.

There are many variations. Some people eat it with brown sugar and grated nutmeg, others with butter and golden syrup. One correspondent wrote, “We always add a good dollop of ‘Oh be joyful’ (rum).”

Amongst the traditions I was told that it must always be eaten by candlelight. (Until recently, grocers in and around Whitby would give the candles as a Christmas present). The candles should be lit by the youngest person present and one old lady wrote to say that she remembers one Christmas Eve when she was five years old watching her mother guide the tiny hand of her new-born baby brother to light the candles. Several people wrote that the door must be locked and that no one is allowed to leave the house that night after it is eaten.

One lady said that it was also eaten ‘when the fair came’ which was probably the patronal festival of the local parish church.

A number of people wrote and said that the reason that it is eaten on Christmas Eve is because it is supposed to be the first food that Mary ate after the birth of Jesus Christ. You may think, as I did, that it is most unlikely that an ancient British dish would be found two thousand years ago in Palestine. But I find from the dictionary that the name frumenty comes from the Latin word 'frumentum' meaning 'corn', so perhaps frumenty originally came here with the Romans. If so, it is not so far-fetched. Palestine was under Roman occupation at roughly the same time as Britain, so frumenty could have made its way to both countries. If, as we suppose, the stable was attached to an inn (possibly frequented by Roman soldiers) it would have been quite natural to take a bowl of such a sustaining mixture to the Mother who had just given birth to a baby. So when you stir your Christmas Pudding (from East to West in honour of the Three Kings), remember that its history could stretch right back to the first Christmas.

December 26th (Boxing Day) is St Stephen's Day.

As the preceding day is Christmas the usual fast is not held:

"Blessed be St Stephen
There's no fast on his even."

At one time St Stephen's Day was spent 'Hunting the Wren' by village boys. It is also the traditional day to give 'tips' to tradesmen and errand boys.

December 31st is Hogmanay, the last day of the year when people gather to see the New Year in. In Scotland it is a bigger festival than Christmas. Traditional recipes are Black Bun and Claggum.

METHOD

Make a rich fruit cake mixture (such as a Christmas cake). Make shortcrust pastry with 1 pound of flour and 8 oz butter and line a large cake tin leaving enough pastry to form a lid. Fill with the cake mixture and put the lid on neatly. Prick the surface and bake for three hours in a moderate oven.

INGREDIENTS

- 1 pint treacle
- ¾ pound brown sugar
- 2 oz butter
- 1 tablespoon vinegar
- 1 teaspoon bicarbonate of soda

Method

Stir the bicarbonate into a little water. Put the other ingredients into a large saucepan and boil to 'hardball' stage. Add the bicarbonate and pour into a greased pan. Stir occasionally and as soon as it is cool enough pull it and twist it into sticks.

There are several other traditional recipes for the new year which you will find under January 1st as the customs for the last day of the old year merge with the first day of the new. The year has come full circle.

Bibliography

Food and Cookery

Aresty, Esther: *The Delectable Past* (1965).
Brothwell, D. & P: *Food in Antiquity* (1969).
Budin, F. M: *Recipes from Ireland* (1966).
Fitzgibbon, Theodora: *A Taste of Wales* (1971).
Grigson, Jane: *English Food* (1974).
Latham, Jean: *The Pleasure of your Company* (1972).
McKendry, Maxime: *Seven Centuries of English Cooking* (1973).
McNeill, F. M: *The Scots' Kitchen* (Glasgow, 1929).
Mead, W. E: *The English Medieval Feast* (1931).
Pullar, Philippa: *Consuming Passions* (1970).
White, Florence: *Good Things in England* (1932).
Wilson, C. Anne: *Food and Drink in Britain* (1973).

Anson, Peter F: *Fisher Folklore* (1965).
Baker, Margaret: *Discovering Christmas Customs and Folklore* (Bucks, 1968).
Gascoigne, Margaret: *Discovering English Customs and Traditions* (Tring, 1969).
Hole, Christina: *English Traditional Customs* (1975).
Hole, Christina: *Saints in Folklore* (1966).
Hottes, A. C: *1001 Christmas Facts and Fancies* (New York, 1937).
Hull, *Folklore of the British Isles* (1954).
Lewis, Don: *Curious and Humorous Customs* (1972).
MacCana, P: *Celtic Mythology* (1970).
McNeill, F. M: *The Silver Bough Vos. 1-3* (1957, '59, '61 Glasgow).
McNeill, F. M: *Hallowe'en* (1970 Edinburgh).
Palmer and Lloyd: *A Year of Festivals* (1972).
Sansom, William: *Christmas* (1968).
Spicer, Dorothy G: *The Book of Festivals* (Detroit 1969).
Weiser, Father F. X: *The Easter Book* (1954).
Weiser, Father F. X: *The Holyday Book* (1957).

Brown, R. L: *A Book of Proverbs* (Devon 1970).
Brown, R. L: *A Book of Superstitions* (Devon 1970).
Burton, Elizabeth: *The Elizabethans at Home* (1958).
Cobbett, William: *Cottage Economy* (1821).
Evans, G. E: *The Pattern under the Plough* (1966).
Kryth, Maymie R: *All about the Months* (New York 1966).
Labarge, M. W: *A Baronial Household of the Thirteenth Century* (1965).
Oxford Dictionary of the Christian Church (1957).
Oxford Dictionary of English Proverbs (Oxford 1970).
Radford, E. and M. A: *Encyclopaedia of Superstitions* (1948).
Trevelyan, G. M: *English Social History* (1944).

Matador